C000109494

There 'tis then:
another miscellany

by the same author:
A Rural Miscellany (2006)

There 'tis then: another miscellany

by
Roscoe Howells

First edition: 2009

© Roscoe Howells

Copyright © by Gwasg Carreg Gwalch 2009
All rights reserved. No part of this publication may be reproduced,
stored in a retrieval system, or transmitted in any form or by
any means, electronic, electrostatic, magnetic tape, mechanical,
photocopying, recording, or otherwise, without prior
permission of the authors of the works herein.

ISBN: 978-1-84527-214-2

Cover image: 'Cymdogion' (*Neighbours*) Aneurin Jones
Cover design: Sian Parri

First published in 2009 by Gwasg Carreg Gwalch
12 Iard yr Orsaf, Llanrwst, Dyffryn Conwy, LL26 0EH.
℡ 01492 642031   ▤ 01492 641502
✆ llyfrau@carreg-gwalch.com   website: www.carreg-gwalch.com

*To those who enjoyed the first effort and urged me
to seek out another collection.*

Foreword

It was way back in 1961 that I first visited Skomer Island and fell in love with the Pembrokeshire islands. It was then too that I picked up a recently published book about Skomer, *Cliffs of Freedom*, by a writer unknown to me, Roscoe Howells. Since then the book has become one of my most prized possessions and the work of Roscoe Howells through his journalism and books has become known to thousands of people. His is the voice of the countryside, the Welsh countryside, which is unique. He writes beautifully and knowingly, covering the whole rural landscape from red tape to wildlife and bureaucrats to shepherds. His pen has many sides to it: humour, anger, happiness and sharpened barbs aimed at those who do not understand, or want to understand, the array of decent and colourful characters who make up our rural farms and villages.

As the farming and political cycles go round, his writing remains fresh, relevant and entertaining. In an age of 'yoof' culture, this book is an antidote to the stream of superficial celebrity rubbish that streams from the media daily. Young and old alike will be amused and informed by one of Wales's best country writers. He has kept the tradition of country writing alive over many years and he shows us that age can bring both wisdom and knowledge with a smile.

When I think of Wales I invariably think of shepherds, sheepdogs, Welsh cakes, mountains, puffins, and yes, the writing of Roscoe Howells.

What a privilege it has been to write this introduction to the latest work of a gifted and good countryman.

Robin Page
April 2008

Acknowledgements

As always, it is difficult to know where to start and where to finish when it comes time to thank so many people. When I was struggling to write my first novel, more than forty years ago, the late Alexander Cordell, who gave me so much practical help and sound advice, said to me, 'No one person writes a book'. And he assured me that no manuscript ever left his house until it had been read and criticised by his friend, Jim Robinson. I am far more fortunate, and indeed richly blessed, because I have my wife to read through my efforts before they are even printed.

Having proof-read thus far I know she would not approve of my saying any more than that, except perhaps to permit me to say an almighty thank you for the debt that all such husbands owe to hugely supportive wives.

There were those over the years who used to draw my attention to any bit of nonsense that was going on here and there, and offer a thought for one more column, which was ever an encouragement when the well was dry. My friends at the Pembrokeshire Records Office are still with us, and still as helpful as they have ever been.

To them all, including that kindred spirit, Robin Page, for his cheerful willingness to write the Foreword, and to do it so generously, what else can be said other than a simple, but truly sincere thank you.

Introduction

I told in *A Rural Miscellany* (2006) how I came to write a column, from 1954-57, under the pen-name 'Barn Owl', for an old Pembrokeshire paper, the *Narberth Weekly News*, the typical post-war betrayal of farming having set in during the 1950s.

From the start of the war, when the nation turned to the farming industry, which had been neglected and betrayed for so long, the evidence was there. First we had the War Agricultural Committees, and bureaucracy took root and flourished.

Churchill went to the country in 1951 with a rousing message to 'set the people free.' The 'War Ags.' were still there, and the first thing he did was to strengthen them and turn them and their increasing hordes of bureaucrats loose on farmers to an extent that would have been a disgrace to a Communist regime in wartime.

Later we were inflicted with Little Harold, followed later by the equally useless Sunny Jim Callaghan, who said he could solve the nation's problems with 'a stroke of the pen'. Those two disasters were interspersed with the reign of the biggest disaster of the lot, Edward Heath, who betrayed the country in the 1970s with his commitment to the so-called European Union.

In 1956 it was announced that civil servants were to have a five-day week. Unfortunately, farmers did not come into this category and, Nature being what it is, are never likely to. They were and are only a small minority of the electorate anyway. The totally misleading untruth of farming subsidies was peddled at will. Never was the truth told that the subsidies were in order to keep down the cost of food to the consumer, and that vast sums were going to the ever-burgeoning hordes of bureaucrats in the ranks of the Min. of Ag. and Fish.

During the pre-war depression in the 1930s farmers had formed their own producers' organisation, the Milk Marketing Board, which had been the salvation of farming. Cometh the war and some of the Board's powers were taken away. When the war was over it was abolished altogether, and the Min. of Ag. and Fish evolved under President Blair to become DEFRA. To those who did not know what the initials stood for, it soon became evident that they meant The Department for the Eradication of Farming and the Rural Areas.

Let it be remembered that many of the old Barn Owl columns, written more than fifty years ago, were trying to put the farming point of view to rural dwellers who did not know what was happening all about them, and who found it difficult to understand that the wealth of a nation lay in what it could produce, and that without a prosperous agriculture there could be no true prosperity.

The pseudonym 'Ben Brock' for the old *Welsh Farm News* came later. The originally harmless badger had not then become the menace it has since become in its increasing thousands, infected by tuberculosis and a danger to the nation's livestock, with urban 'do-gooders' failing to understand the need for positive action to be taken to control the menace.

In trying now to put together this anthology, and reading through what was written so long ago, apart from remembering the political and economic background of the time, I think I should explain that many of the repetitions and ungrammatical phrases were those which were much-beloved of some of the orators of the day, and to quote them was no more than trying to take the old Mickey out of some of them. Such turns of phrase as 'One and all', 'Each and every one of us', 'Like I said', 'As I said', or 'If I may say.' And yes, that great favourite, 'I won't put it no higher.' Nowadays there would be more of 'What I would like to say,'and 'I have to say', because it's all about 'moving the goalposts' on a 'level playing field'. It should not be too challenging to think up a few more.

The *There 'tis then* pieces came later in a local paper as one of a number of *As I See It* columns, which eventually came to an end in due season.

Still, as the farmer said to the land-girl, "We had a lot of fun, no harm done, and thanks for the memory."

Welsh Farm News, 5 October 1957

I was reading in this *Welsh Farm News* paper a week or two ago about this bloke Turner from the National Farmers Union telling the tale over there in Ireland about efficiency and all that. Bit of all right that was. Only he doesn't know the half of it.

One of the factors that could and should contribute to this lowering of the costs of production lark, according to Sir James. '. . . is the efficiency of those industries which supply agriculture with goods and services valued currently at some £800 million a year.' Now maybe you don't understand a lot of big words like that, so perhaps I'd better explain what he was getting at.

It's about a character whose tractor broke down, and one wet day he tried to get it going again. And this character was known as a small man – who has many more problems than anybody else – and this little chap had plenty of problems as you shall see.

Well, this little chap pulled the tractor abroad [which is a good Pembrokeshire term] because he was a handy sort of cove like that, and he didn't belong to the sort of union that would stop a chap pulling a tractor abroad just because he didn't hold a tractor-puller-abroader's card. As soon as he'd pulled the things to bits he found out what was wrong. And that was the valve springs.

So what should this chap do then but up and away, and on to his bike and off to go for the nearest telephone box. There was a fair bit of performance with this contraption about a button which had to be pressed, and no-one was very clear about what was going on. But in the end he got through to his local garage where the bloke was a pal of his and would know all about these valve springs.

So that was that, and the little chap was very

pleased, because he'd ordered the valve springs from his pal and not from one of the big dealers he bought off sometimes when he couldn't avoid it. For the one lot left him a plough one day when he wasn't there, and it was the wrong one, and he only used it sometimes, and they wouldn't fetch it back, but kept on sending him bills which he said point blank he wouldn't pay – but he had to in the end to help pay for this outfit's marvellous new show-room.

The other lot were a bunch of sharks and very stupid, and the last time they'd had some bother was about some driving-bars that kept breaking and they found they'd been sending the wrong ones for there was a letter J under the grease which they hadn't seen before, and which probably meant they were all right thank you, Jack, as long as the little chap paid for the driving bars. Which he refused to do. But this lot also had a new show-room and they had a good solicitor. He paid.

Now this chap was more pleased than somewhat about cutting out the other two, but eventually the springs didn't come, so he jumps on his bike again and off he goes all the way to see this pal of his and plays pop.

This pal says about a lot of things that have happened that don't concern Sir James Turner any more than the bloke not getting very good service on the telephone. But he takes a bit of interest and says he will see into this business.

Sure enough, a few days later, here comes a parcel of corrugated paper and cardboard and some of the new fancy tape sticking it all together, and inside are the valve springs. It is not raining at the time, but this chap is now wanting to use his tractor, so he has to go and put them in straightaway, and he finds they are the wrong size and too big. Not much too big. But too big all the same. Which, of course, makes him very cross.

So off on the bike he goes to telephone his garage pal who blames it on to the firm who'd mucked it up about the driving bars, through whom he has to order, and they blame it on to the lot who'd done it on him about the plough, for they were the main dealers and had really sent them on.

Then everybody said the springs would do, for it said in the book they would fit this particular model. Which was quite right, and so they couldn't understand it until somebody had the bright idea to look in another book, and then they found that those were not the ones they'd sent on anyway.

So then they said that if the farmer would pay for the telephone calls and the bus fare they would put the right ones on the bus, and he agreed to do this because he was now desperate to get his tractor going.

So now you will understand why Sir James Turner was saying a word in its place back over, and you will also know all about lowering the costs of production.

Welsh Farm News, 26 October 1957

There was an article in *Welsh Farm News* some little time ago about an attempt being made to establish a colony of Canada geese in Pembrokeshire.

I am interested in this sort of project and in birds generally, and although I don't reckon to know a powerful lot about it, that doesn't prevent a chap from being interested.

It so happens also that I have recently been reading a book called *Jack Miner and the Birds*. It is an American book and just about the best on birds that has ever come my way. For one thing, it was so obviously written by a man with his heart in the right place. And much of his life was spent in dealing with his beloved Canada geese. The story of how he became interested in the geese and his subsequent experiences with them makes fascinating and absorbing reading.

A keen sportsman as a young man, he spent so much time hunting the geese that he became familiar with their ways. It became obvious to him that they knew him for an enemy, and he reasoned that, with their highly developed intelligence, they could also learn to know him as a friend.

He set out to prove his friendship and succeeded in full measure. His little holding near the shores of Lake Ontario in Canada became the visiting place of thousands of Canada geese in their migratory passage, and of other birds that called on him for sanctuary.

As time passed he so learned to love the birds that, for years before his death, he never took a gun in his hand except to destroy their enemies.

Yet he did not turn against the principle of taking birds for good. His philosophy was simple, and based on possibly the first game law ever published. It is to be found in verses six and seven of the twenty-second chapter of Deuteronomy: 'If a bird's nest chance to be

14

before thee in any tree, or on the ground, whether they be young ones, or eggs, and the dam sitting upon the young, or upon the eggs, thou shalt not take the dam with the young: but thou shalt in any wise let the dam go, and take the young to thee: that it may be well with thee, and that thou mayest prolong thy days.'

With the passing of the gin trap and consequently the rabbit, many farmers are breeding a few pheasants and partridges. With the passing of the big estates, and with many farmers owning their own farms and their own shooting rights for the first time they are taking a more active interest in game than ever before. And I know that many of them take as much delight in seeing the birds about the place as ever they do in the amount of shooting they provide.

Now the birds were put there by the Great Provider for all of us. For those, in the vast majority, who would enjoy the beauty of their flight and every movement, and for the small minority who find sport in shooting them, or those who need to take them for food.

And the point is made that if the shooter approached the question with a sound business-like outlook he would greatly increase the stock of birds to his own advantage. Nor would he be depriving those who love them of the pleasure which is also theirs by right.

The approach is simple enough. 'Thou shalt let the dam go that it may be well with thee.'

There is, without doubt, room for a great deal of serious thinking on the subject as one which could reap a rich reward. But of them all it is possible that the establishing of a colony of Canada geese is as likely to give the most satisfaction. For of the geese it has been written: 'When the north-east wind blows at dawn, and the flood-tides creep in across the mud, it is the sudden call of the geese, half-heard above the roar of wind and waves, that brings the greatest thrill of all. When the full moon rises over the marsh at dusk, and the creeks are brimful; when eyes are strained to see which way the bubbles float, so that one may know if full sea is past or yet to come, it is the call of the geese which makes one's heart leap.'

That, to my mind, is the real spirit of these great mysterious birds that come to our shores in darkness out of the frozen northland.

How nice to have them with us all the time.

But, 'Thou shalt let the dam go that it may be well with thee.'

---

22 November 1956

Telling the world

The ploughman thought he was pretty good. I don't know what the farmer thought, but for one reason or another he wasn't at all keen on the ploughman's idea of entering at a ploughing match.

But the ploughman insisted. So the farmer finally threw cold water over the whole idea.

"Don't you be a so-and-so fool," says he. "As 'tis, only thee and me knows thou cas'n't plough. But go thee there and every bugger'll know."

I should think there's a moral in it somewhere.

Welsh Farm News, 16 November 1957

So then, it falls to me to write to the Editor of Wales' new paper claiming to have heard the first cuckoo of the season.

This is one of the most ancient and time-honoured customs known to mankind. Every year they do it, and Editors thrive on it. How nice, therefore, to be the first with the claim in a brand new paper. Others there will be in other years. But it won't be quite the same. For this here is my bird. And it's in the bag. As early as November.

And this particular cuckoo has been calling loud and clear, for all to hear, in high places. In places where we expect, and usually get, much good common-sense for all the chance moments of mental aberration. I refer now to the Council of the NFU which, report has it, was recently confronted by a resolution from the Caernarvonshire Executive that summertime be extended to November.

That such an effort should have come from Wales. Dear, dear me. Well, well, well. Whatever shall we hear next?

As far as I know some fool started this lark about 1916 to get the people out of bed an hour earlier. Well, maybe if you can't get them out of bed any other way and they're daft enough to fall for this stunt, then they deserve all they have coming to them. However, the war over, as so often happens in the case of something filched from the people in time of stress in the name of national urgency, this heathen practice was allowed to continue. More to our shame, we have remained, and shall probably continue, too feeble-minded and jelly-kneed to do anything at all about it.

Every election time we return to power the same ninny-witted politicians or their equally ninny-witted opponents who consider the whole burning question to be so devoid of consequence as to be allowed to ignore it in their manifestos which can, for all other ills, be regarded as the complete panacea.

Yet, as I say, these are the people amongst whom we share our cherished votes. We do not chuck bombs in letter boxes. Neither do we write rude words upon the wall.

With the dew not off the corn when things begin to move, it means that the already harassed farmer has to pay one hour's overtime at the end of the day for work his man doesn't want to do. Cows are brought from the field for milking so early in the afternoon that they probably wonder whether to come back again at dusk. Children are called in from their play before they are ready to go to bed at night, and can't be dragged from bed to go to school in the morning. It makes them irritable and, I believe, has an injurious effect on their health.

The Good Lord gave us the joy of sunrise and dewy morn to enjoy them if we would. Some of us have drunk this glory to the full. Others maybe less often. Yet now, those who would partake of this same glory in splendid isolation are thwarted by this crazy stunt which inveigles the morons to emerge from between their inviting linen an hour before they should, and goodness knows how long before they want to. And this is done because these same clods, who can't get up in the morning, are glad to find there is an extra hour of daylight to be enjoyed and think they have had something for nothing.

For it is symptomatic of the lunatic times in which we live that large droves of the common rabble really do believe that something for nothing is not only possible, but theirs by right. Poor fools. The idea seems to be that if you can get them out of bed you might get them to work, provided that their shop stewards will permit their indulgence in this anti-social vice.

I also understand there are nations producing about twice as much as we do without the impediment of this self-inflicted torment. I can't think of anything more at the moment, but I have no doubt it will boil up again in due course.

We badgers are harmless enough in our way, and friendly souls if given the opportunity. But we do not suffer fools gladly.

'That summertime be extended to November.'

Do they really believe the days would be less cold and the grass any greener?

Exactly what can you say about such a resolution from a section of an industry which suffers most from this buffleheaded, unwarranted and totally unnecessary interference with the natural scheme of things?

It is a comfort to know that the nonsense was not supported by Headquarters of the NFU.

Welsh Farm News, 21 December 1957

In the lives of all of us there are milestones which we remember and which mean something to us. Milestones to which we look forward, which we shall not see again but which, often enough, look uncommonly like the ones that went before. At some of them we decide that we shall try to do better between there and the next one and make a better showing along the road. We like to look back, too, sometimes and remember what has gone before. To remember chiefly what is good in life.

Such is the milestone we now approach as Christmas draws near. It is a milestone common to all of us, and the first to occur in the life of our paper.

It might not, therefore, be out of place to rest awhile and ponder on the background of what it's all about, and the message it unfailingly tries to bring. It is a message which, perhaps not as much as might be realised, means something just a little extra to those who till the soil and tend the stock.

For once upon a time, long, long, ago, a child was born, which in itself is cause for gladness. Whilst life endures, such an occasion will be marked by rejoicing. Yet this was no ordinary occasion and no ordinary child. This indeed was a promised child, and the glad tidings were of a babe that was to save mankind. So that angels sang of Glory to God, and of peace and goodwill towards men.

Once again we find ourselves about to celebrate this very special birthday. We bring to mind by our reading and our songs of praise that the birthplace was in a manger, in a stable. Which we might consider odd, unless we accept that human nature probably wasn't very different then from now, because officialdom had decreed that the people should be counted. For this purpose officialdom had called the people together into one place and, after the manner of their kind, had failed to make adequate provision for their comfort.

So that it came to pass that the Saviour of Mankind arrived, without fuss and without bother, amongst the beasts of the field. The people of the day, being no more ready to recognise the truth and the obvious than we are today, knew not of the wonderful happening in their midst. The news of it was entrusted to ordinary simple men who lived by the land. To shepherds with their flocks. Men who kept faithful and patient watch over their sheep through the cold, clear night.

To these men was entrusted the news and they questioned not. In simple faith they arranged for some of their number to remain with their flocks, whilst the rest went in search of the promised Christ. And they had but their faith to guide them.

Why this should have been, with an ordinary cattle crib, and men of the soil being thus honoured, I do not know. I only know that it was so.

Yet, for all the rejoicing and the promise of peace, and the sacrifice this babe was one day to be called on to make for the sake of mankind, it hardly seems to have worked out that way. And I do not think that we need search far beyond ourselves to find the reason, for we seem to have done, and continue to do, so little about it.

With apparently no thought, we complain of the cost of living, that this, that and the other are scarce, or that we can't afford them.

Whilst we do this we seem to consider it right and proper to support vast numbers who produce nothing. At the same time we dissipate our effort and honest toil on the costly production of armaments, which we are told are necessary in order to ensure peace on earth.

We do these things because there is so little real goodwill on earth. We cannot trust each other. So we cannot hope to find that selfsame peace which, we are told, necessitates this preparation against destruction.

Yet the other side of the bargain is being kept. For could we but learn to direct our efforts down peaceful channels, in search of things that matter, the good things of the earth are there in abundance and for the taking.

Such then is Christmas and the cause for our rejoicing. We remember the message that it brings and we think of others. We give thanks and we extend our good wishes.

Whilst all those who possibly can will spend Christmas Day in the manner of their choosing, in worship or in bed, eating, drinking, romping with the children or in a dozen and one different ways, we might remember those to whom this Day is just another turn in the wheel of grinding at it.

Those whose job it is to milk the cows at least twice a day and to tend the need of the dumb animals in their care. The lorry-drivers who – because someone has to do it – come round to collect the milk, and those at the other end who – because it will not keep – deliver it to the doors of those who are enjoying their well-earned rest. The vets who will be called out to the inevitable case of milk-fever or the difficult calving, and who will set out cheerfully because they know that time, tide and rigor mortis wait for no man.

There are those, too, who, whilst performing these tasks, will give thanks for their health and strength, and remember those who would be glad to be doing them if only they had theirs.

So we shall remember the sick and those who minister to them and seek to bring comfort. Especially shall we remember those who are away from their loved ones. And we shall remember those who grow old and are alone and in need. In a moment of the spirit of Christmas we might even bestir ourselves to seek them out and do something about it.

We could all, I have no doubt, name many things which we believe would be good for mankind. And we cannot have them, for reasons of pounds, shillings and pence. Yet the whole lot put together pale into insignificance beside the rate at which we squander our substance on armaments.

So that my own particular wish is for peace on earth and goodwill to all men.

Then, when we have remembered everybody and everything, may we remember once again what Christmas really means to us and why we celebrate it.

May we honestly try to remember the message it tries to bring to us year after year, and keep it with us until Christmas comes again.

Could we but do this, I think things might well go much better with us.

MERRY CHRISTMAS.

Welsh Farm News, 18 January 1958

Judging by reports from various parts of the country it rather looks as if the rabbit is likely to remain with us for some time to come.

When myxomatosis was annihilating our rabbit population a few years ago we fondly imagined that we would be able to clear up the few which remained and write off the rabbit as a back number.

The virtual disappearance of our rabbits was so sudden that a period was inevitable in which the balance of nature could readjust itself. Buzzards, for example, which had come to regard rabbits as their staple diet, had to turn elsewhere for their food, and have now become much fewer in numbers in a state of affairs where less food has been available to them.

But the consequences have not been as dire as some predicted, whilst the benefits have been immeasurable. The pressing need at the moment, therefore, would appear to be to keep the rabbits to an absolute minimum. The surest way to do this would be by the maximum utilization of our old friend the ferret.

We read in *Welsh Farm News* some little time ago that Mr. David Perkins, the well-known Pembrokeshire agriculturalist, had cleared his two farms of rabbits before the war by allowing the unemployed of the neighborhood to ferret on his land.

On the islands of Skomer and Skokholm off the West Coast of Pembrokeshire rabbits have always been numerous and, in the life and economy of these islands, rabbits have played an important part since very early days. Interesting figures are available of the income from rabbits during the 14th century, together with how many rabbits were allowed per ferreter and so on. The point is that ferrets were used.

And so thorough were they in their work that from time to time the islands had to be restocked with rabbits. And this was so even though there are none of the rabbits' natural enemies, such as weasels or foxes, on the islands, so that the rabbits can, and do, increase there very quickly.

Some time ago I made the point in this column that the steel trap had been the biggest single contributory cause in the alarming increase of rabbits in this country.

I think indeed that it should not be at all difficult to make out a very good case for getting down to the job of ferreting right away. Instead of which, however, there is much talk about gas (poison), grants, compulsion and all sorts of things.

It is possibly not surprising that nothing very inspiring has yet come from the Ministry of Agriculture.

Maybe they feel they don't know enough about the job. But I can't for the life of me see why the Livestock Officers shouldn't take a hand. After all is said and done, if they are supposed to be able to say on sight that a particular bull of any one of a dozen or more different breeds is just no good, they surely ought to be able to recognise a good ferret if they saw one.

Welsh Farm News, 25 January 1958

Writing last week on rabbits and ferrets I referred to the balance of nature. We heard rather much of this you may remember when myxomatosis was taking its toll.

Usually the people who talked about it implied or asserted that the introduction and spreading of the disease were the work of man's own hands.

Many of the same people do not approve of attempts to eliminate the rabbit entirely from the countryside. Some of them would claim also to be religious or God-fearing people, and they deplore what they regard as any interference with the balance of nature. Yet I think we would be in a rather sorry state were we to expect God and/or Nature to do it all.

Rather like the story of the sailor who returned from the sea and took over an allotment – something he had often dreamed of doing as he had sailed across endless stretches of ocean and journeyed to foreign parts.

Now he had his heart's desire. The allotment had been untenanted and neglected for years. Brambles and nettles held undisputed sway. But the sailor was undaunted and went to work. He cut. He burned. He dug. And in the fullness of time he saw the first uncertain crops show rich with promise. Ceaselessly and happily he worked away. Then one summer evening as he busied himself with caring for these same crops the vicar chanced along and stopped for a chat.

'You have some very nice crops here,' said the parson.

'Not too bad at all,' said the sailorman

'Nice potatoes. Good cabbages, and the peas are very promising.'

'Aye, not bad at all,' agreed the gardener happily.

'Indeed, Mister Jones,' said the parson, warming to his theme, 'it's wonderful to behold what you and the

Almighty have done together on this piece of land.'

'Aye, I suppose it is really, vicar,' came the reply, 'but I'd like you to have seen it when the Almighty had it on his own.'

They were both right for, in this business of Nature, God and man are partners. It has been so since time began, and the promise is clear for all to see. I would refer you to verses 26–30 of the first Chapter of Genesis. 'And God said, Let us make man in our own image, after our likeness: and let them have dominion over the fish of the sea, and over the fowl of the air, and over the cattle, and over all the earth, and over every creeping thing that creepeth upon the earth.'

I don't think we need to go into it too deeply to appreciate the sense of it all. As you journey through the rich valleys of Breconshire on into the rolling acres of Herefordshire and see those handsome herds of red, white-faced beef cattle, does any anyone imagine for one moment that they were always there?

No, they are there as a result of the skill and care over countless generations of breeders improving their stock to meet man's requirements. They are there because God in His wisdom 'gave man dominion over all.'

In the same way man has developed some cows to give large quantities of milk, and some cows to give very rich milk.

Because God gave him 'dominion over all' man has developed various breeds of poultry to lay eggs or provide good table birds. And God, having given him 'dominion over all', man would be all kinds of a fool if he failed to destroy the foxes, hawks, rats or other thieving predators that come to take his chickens from him.

Because God gave him 'dominion over all' man has developed many things from small beginnings. Beautiful flowers, lovely shrubs, improved potatoes, peas, cabbage, apples and all manner of fruits. He has made tremendous strides with improved strains of corn and grasses.

Oh, yes. As I was saying. The rabbit knows all about these improved strains of corn and grasses and cabbage and lettuce and also the bark of young trees.

So, because God gave him 'dominion over all', man had better go and do something about it.

And, balance of nature or not, that, dear friends, is the answer to that one.

23 June 1955

Barn Owl

"Now then, my boy," says teacher, "supposing I lent your father £100 and he promised to pay me back £30 when he'd sold his early potatoes, £30 when he'd sold his corn, and £30 when he'd sold his sugar beet, how much would he be owing me at the end of the year?"

"£100, sir," says Tommy.

"Indeed," says teacher. "It's obvious you don't know your arithmetic."

"No, sir," says Tommy," You don't know father!"

Welsh Farm News, 25 June 1960

'Twould seem to be a strange world in which we live. The regular readers of this column (both of you) will recall that from time to time I have made mention of the rather antiquated approach we have to our problems of water supplies, conservation thereof, and so on and so forth.

Of recent years farmers have been coerced as far as possible into abandoning perfectly good private water supplies on the grounds that they couldn't possibly be as healthy as the tepid, chlorinated stuff that can occasionally be induced to trickle though the hopelessly overloaded water mains.

Vast quantities of beautiful water have therefore been allowed to run to waste even in time of the most serious drought.

Enterprising farmers here and there are showing an increasing tendency to use this water for irrigation. But this, too, would seem to be wrong, and alarm is being expressed at the way this is likely to interfere with the nation's water supplies.

Water, water everywhere and not a drop to drink.
Councils, Councils everywhere and none with brains to think.

Welsh Farm News, 2 July 1960

A few of you have very kindly been enquiring lately as to how the farming is going these days. I wouldn't like to say there's a great deal to report and, in any case, can't imagine that more than the odd happening could be of interest to you.

It might, however, be worth recording that after ten years of all silage we are, sheep-like, going back to some haymaking. I believe it's the done thing these days. Not that I've got anything against silage, but having read some place lately about it being a free country, I said to myself, 'What the hell.' So I decided on making a bit of hay again.

Obviously, having finished mowing the first field, it came to rain following a thunderstorm and, up to the time of writing, the rain continues. Still, not to worry. It doesn't mean that haymaking is out.

What has been done so far is against the rules of the modern technique. Too big an acreage cut together, for one thing. But we'll talk about that another day. Another thing that was not in accordance with present-day techniques has been inability to start tedding* from the word 'go'. Largely this has been due to the 'settling down' process of some of the new implements it has been necessary to acquire.

One of these, by the way, is so good that it is the standard by which its numerous imitators are now judged. I rather care for that. The rest of the directions on the glossy little book that came with it are not so specific.

The worst torment, however, was the setting up of the new mower. I had, you will understand, been talked into acquiring one of these delightful new toys (mounted) in view of a satisfactory offer for a much older (trailer) which had undeniably seen better days.

Having been typically foolish in failing to insist on a

thorough demonstration before final acceptance as it were, it was inevitable that 'the man' – like the manager of the zoo in Stanley Holloway's immortal *Albert and the Lion* – 'had to be sent for'.**

Upon my return from devious travelling thither and thence on your behalf I found the typical mechanic (henceforth to be referred to as T.M.) in the final stages of completing the operations necessary for the successful setting in motion of one mower.

This had obviously been accomplished by the sawing off and cutting asunder of various pieces, pipes and odds and bobs to the utter bewilderment of one bemused badger (obviously to be referred to hereafter as B.B.).

In reply, therefore, to the question referred to at the beginning, as to how the farming was going these days, I do trust you will consider the following little conversation piece to be worth recording:-

B.B. – How's it going on here?

T.M. – She ought to go now.

B.B. – But what's this bit of tube?

T.M. – What tube?

B.B. – This tube I've just trodden on.

T.M. – You mean that round piece with a hole in it?

B.B. – Yes, that one.

T.M. – That's off the what-you-call.

B.B. – That's what I was wondering.

T.M. – What?

B.B. – What what?

T.M. – What was you wondering?

B.B. – I was wondering about the what-you-call and wouldn't you want it again some time maybe?

T.M. – No, I don't want'n.

B.B. – But don't you think I might?

T.M. – Yes, you might.

B.B. – Then how will I manage without it?

T.M. – You can use the other what-you-call.

B.B. – Which do you call the other what-you-call?

T.M. – That thing underneath the other thing.

B.B. – But according to the book of instructions there's supposed to be a chain to stop that thing spragging the what-you-call.

T.M. – You don't take no notice of that.

B.B. – Why not?

T.M. – They makes 'em like that in case you haves some other make of tractor.

B.B. – But I haven't got another make of tractor. I've got this one. That's why I bought this mower to have them both the same so as it would fit.

T.M. – It does fit now.

B.B. – Yes, but only because you made that pipe shorter.

T.M. – Yes, that's how I made 'n shorter.***

B.B. – But what about the safety regulations?

T.M. – You don't take no notice of them. They're daft.

B.B. – Well what about this book of instructions?

T.M. – You don't take no notice of that.

B.B. – How not?

T.M. – That's for the old model.

B.B. – But how do they say that if it isn't right?

T.M. – Well that's the book which comes with the machine.

B.B. – You mean it isn't the proper book for this machine?

T.M. – It's nearly the same apart from the what-you-call.

B.B. – But what's this piece you've been cutting off at the top?

T.M. – That's the piece that sticks out there.

B.B. – Yes, I can see that. But why saw it off?

T.M. – We always saws'n off.

B.B. – Why do you always saw it off?

T.M. – It sticks out too far.

B.B. – Then why do they make them like that?

T.M.– They always makes 'em like that.

B.B. – Who always makes them like that?

T.M. – The makers.

B.B. – Have they always put it on there?

T.M. – Oh, yes. They've always put'n on there.

B.B. – Oh, I see. They've always put it on there?

T.M. – Yes, they've always put'n on there.

B.B. – I wonder why?

T.M. – I don't know. But they always have, and we always saws'n off.

B.B. – Go and have a drink with me, fellah. I must go in and write a little piece about efficiency.

---

* Tedding: to spread or turn, as new mown grass at haymaking time.
** Stanley Holloway the actor (he played Eliza Doolittle's father in *My Fair Lady*) also recorded monologues. Perhaps the most famous was the story about the couple who took their son to the zoo, where he was eaten by a lion named Wallace. 'The keeper were quite nice about it, and said, 'What a nasty mishap. Are you sure that it's your boy he's eaten?' Pa said, 'Am I sure? Here's his cap!' **The manager had to be sent for**, he came and he said, 'What's to do?' Mother said, 'Yon lion's ate Albert, and him in his Sunday clothes too.'
*** Pembrokeshire people usually say 'how when they mean 'why'.

Welsh Farm News, 4 March 1961

I'm not sure whether it was my old pal Billy Shakespeare or I myself when in my cups who once said, 'It's an East wind that blows nobody any good.'

Just as certainly as at this time of year we have to endure it, so also at this time of year do we see increasing numbers of lorries loaded with hay trundling along the roads. To me they are always a depressing sight for I always say to myself, 'There's another poor so-and-so in trouble.' 'Tis a hard world, friends, when the cows are looking round at the cowshed door whenever you go in, and you don't know where the next forkful is coming from.

Certainly when you come to dole out a ton of hay it goes nowhere. And, as often as not, the fellow who is forced to buy hay is the one who can least afford it.

If you can buy it for cash money off the field in the summer that's one thing, but to go looking for it now is a load of a very different quality.

I sometimes wonder, with transport charges amounting to what they do, to what extent the price could be reduced if there was some co-ordination about the whole business. How many people buy hay at X and transport it to Y, whilst at the same time someone is buying hay at Y and transporting it to X?

I recently saw the fantastic sight of a lorry load of hay too high to go under a railway bridge. It had come a distance of 25 miles and had another 15 miles to go. The other side of the bridge there was another fellow stuck with another load.

He had come from within a couple of miles of the other chap's destination, and he had another 20 miles to go in the direction from which the other chap had come.

In cold figures it meant that the two loads had travelled between them about 70 miles, when 10 would more than have covered it. To say nothing of the return journeys of the empty lorries. One of these days I must see about starting a campaign to get this operation placed on the list for increased efficiency.

And if I don't make any more impression than with the fools who believe in summertime I won't be spoiling much fun for the hay merchants.

* * *

Quite recently I had occasion to call at a roadside café for a quick, frugal, greasy, but much-needed meal.

Just as I was about to depart, an individual, identifiable loosely as a 'speed-cop', came in, ordered a cup of tea, just like a human being, took it to a table, sat down, took off his cap very polite, lit up a cigarette, and settled back to enjoy life generally.

I don't think even our motoring correspondent could ever have been presented with such a heaven-sent opportunity. Come to think of it, maybe it has never happened before in the annals of British motoring.

He was just washing down the first lungful of smoke with the second mouthful of tea when I tapped him on the shoulder. Politely, of course, as is my wont, but firmly nevertheless.

As he looked at me I remember thinking that he gave the impression that he might have been a good husband and a kind father. But it would have taken much greater considerations than that to cloud the issue.

'Excuse me, sir', says I, and I emphasised the 'sir'. 'Excuse me, sir', I says, 'but this is a chance I've been waiting for all my life. The chance to ask a copper please to come and move his motor car.'

I had noticed that he had parked his car in about the only available space outside in such a way as to impede my lawful egress from the premises.

35

He saw the joke and enjoyed it, but was far more apologetic than he need have been. Then he explained that it had simply been the only place left to him, and he knew he would only be a few minutes. So I says, 'That's all right, fellah, but just remember that the next time you've got some poor fish like me on the end of the line.'

He promised to do that small thing and parked his car very tidy as I was driving away. I hope that he keeps his promise, and I hope that either you or I will reap the benefit.

But I have my doubts.

Welsh Farm News, 1 July 1961

The time of year is at hand when wasps, picnickers and other kindred torments known to mankind can be expected to descend upon us.

Some areas are afflicted worse than others, but no-one is completely immune. Inmates of the National Parks have oft times been known to bear witness to the extent of their sufferings.

There are those to be found who, either from an inherent sense of faith in humanity or for some nebulous idea that one day all prayers will be answered, fondly believe that, if they go on campaigning long enough and loud enough, workable legislation will one day be introduced to curb the doings of the litter louts.

Nebulous also happens to be a very good word and means without foundation. Everybody knows there is an excessive use of paper in our modern civilisation, and the zeal with which even the most disinterested shop assistant will wrap the most ordinary purchase in yards of inadequate wrapping is unbelievable. Even without the aiding and abetting of the shop assistants, the manufacturers have already played their part with cardboard, cartons, tin-foil, cellophane and all the rest of it.

When you come to think of it, it is not entirely easy not to leave litter about the place. Especially when there ain't always no litter basket ready to hand not nohow.

There was rather a classic example of this in London about four years ago when the Parish Councils held a National Conference. It lasted a couple of days and there were many impassioned speeches calling for action because the Parish Councils are very active bodies and do not take kindly to litter being left all over the place. Near the end a lady delegate took command of the rostrum and let 'em have it good and strong, left, right and centre.

To put them in the right frame of mind she told them the classic old story of the teacher trying to set the feet of her young class on the right road towards keeping Britain tidy.

She had found a little pile of toffee papers on the floor in the corner of the cloakroom. So when the class was duly assembled she made mention of this and delivered a little sermon calculated to touch the hearts of her young listeners and arouse their finer little feelings. Then, having been studying all about the modern trend in Psychology, she said that no more would be said about it if the culprit would go out and pick up the toffee papers. And so that no-one would know who it was they would all close their eyes for three minutes.

Which said, they did. They all closed their eyes. Then they heard the pitter patter of little footsteps, the opening and closing of a door, and then the returning pitter patter of the little footsteps.

So teacher said it was all right and they could now all open their eyes. Then she went out to the cloakroom to see if the toffee papers had been picked up. They hadn't. But there was now another pile in the other corner with a hastily scribbled note, 'The phantom strikes again!' And if it wasn't toffee papers the first time you heard the story, the moral is sill the same and it also proves that you don't mix with such nice people as I do.

The Conference greeted this with laughter and great good humour, and then the lady delegate upset them rather by asking them to take a look under their seats on the way out and witness the filth, which for all their piousness, they were leaving behind them in the way of fag ends and empty packets after two days of resolutions.

As a result of the Conference, resolutions on litter were sent to one and all. But by the time the next National Conference was held three years later they still hadn't had the brains to provide trays to alleviate some of the ash-ridden problem.

As I said when I started, in some areas the problem is worse than others. By the seaside. there is no hope. I explained to you that nebulous means without foundation, and there are already a great number of nebulous women about the place this year. I am sure about this because they are wide in the beam and would look less horrible in their shorts if they wore corsets. But indeed they are extremely nebulous.

In spite of these eyesores, many people rush to the seaside in order to leave a great deal of litter behind them. But I happen to know that, however much you preach, there is no hope. Only very recently I was driving through a built-up area with the sort of revenue from rates that would make our Parish Council have heart failure. Along the road was being driven a mechanically propelled vehicle emblazoned with the heraldic trappings of the Corporation. Its function was, by means of a contrivance most ingenious, to gather up into its nethermost depths or guts all the debris which befouled the highway.

Let me say at once that it was doing the job in a way of which its makers could be proud. As I drew nigh I saw that the driver of this drudge's aid was in the act of finishing off the contents of a packet of crisps. And as he did so he rolled up the empty paper packet and, with an air of the utmost unconcern, flicked it through the open window out into the middle of the road.

As usual it is unfortunately a fact that I know what I am talking about and recognise the problem as being both human and economic. In an effort to be constructive, however, and entirely without prejudice, I offer this column's usual prize of a leather medal to the writer of the best letter on how to make a pound note do the work of a penny on a crowded promenade.

The Editor's decision will be final.

---

4 October 1956

Hypothetic diary

January – Buy a little place in the country. Put a man in to look after it.

February – Man writes to say that, owing to the floods, the neighbourhood is very damp and unhealthy.

March – Man writes to say that the meadow and garden are under water.

April – Man writes to say that there is six foot of water in the barn and that they are using the cart as a rowing boat.

May – Man writes to say that part of the cowshed has been washed away.

June – Man writes to say that all the farm stock, except for two homing pigeons, have been drowned.

July – Go down to the little place in the country.

August – Escape through the bedroom window in the cart being used as a boat and send pigeons out with distress signals.

September – In bed with pneumonia.

October – Man writes to say that floods are out worse than ever.

November – Pigeons return with message that man has been drowned.

December – Try to sell little place in the country.

Welsh Farm News, 12 August 1961

I am wishing to tell you this week about the very sad story of a ram lamb because I tell you last week that I will be doing that small thing. And maybe you notice that if I sometimes say that maybe I will tell you about so-and-so or something or other one day, then maybe I will and maybe I won't. But if I say I am going to tell you, then you can be sure that you have no option other than to hear about it.

Now this story concerns a character who takes a ram lamb to the show. He does not intend to do this in the first place, but he is got at by his neighbours because he has such an outstanding ram lamb. And as he has some cows and this and that going to the show he decides to send the ram lamb in the same lorry.

Unfortunately there is a character by the name of Billy Shots who gets to hear about this. There is a story once that he gets his name because he is philosophizing one night with his friends when he is in his cups and is interrupted by the cuckoo coming out of the clock to announce the hour.

So he gets the gun, which is in fact an old revolver, and the cuckoo being due out again a dozen times at midnight, he decides to put a stop to this nonsense and let him have it right between the first oo and the second cuck. But this story is a very great slander generally, because he is such a poor shot he will not hit a haystack even if he is aiming at it and only manages to smash the clock.

And I happen to know that he gets his name because of a time when he is at a show and having some food when the waitress asks him does he fancy some stewed gooseberries. To which he replies, 'No indeed thank you, girl. Those old gooseberries do go through me like shots.'

Well, being generally on the make, Billy Shots decides to do something about this ram lamb, because

41

his brother-in-law offers him a split in any business he can get for him which is handling compression-packed OPO, the new wonder cleaner guaranteed to wash black sheep whiter than white.

So a few nights before the show he gets at this ram lamb and turns him into the barn where there is a drum of coal-tar paint which has just been opened, and amidst the resultant confusion the ram lamb gets in a very bad mess whatever and his chances for the show are reduced to somewhere.

But the very next morning who should turn up but Billy Shots' brother-in-law, and he talks this character who has the ram lamb into buying a gallon of OPO on the spot and also persuades him that his ram lamb will then be eligible as a late entry paying double entry fee for the whiter than white fleece competition sponsored by OPO, the new wonder cleaner guaranteed to wash black sheep whiter than white.

From all of which you will gather that this character who has the ram lamb is extremely simple and should not at any time be allowed out without his mammy. Even so, they make a very good job of washing the ram lamb, in spite of the great shortage of water at the time, which is a great unsolicited testimonial to OPO, the new wonder cleaner guaranteed to wash black sheep whiter than white. Unfortunately his fleece is now so fluffy that when they go to put him in the lorry they find that with the cows and this and that, there just isn't enough room. So Billy Shots' brother-in-law sells this character who owns the ram lamb a new Clippo hand-shearer guaranteed to trim white fleeces closer than close. Which same it certainly now does.

Which is about all there is to tell except that the ram lamb doesn't get a prize although this character's aunt who goes to chapel every Sunday and sometimes plays the organ thinks it is the prettiest little lamb in the whole show.

Now you must please yourself whether you believe this story to be true or not, and far be it from me to express an opinion. But certainly other people have heard it, if only a garbled version, which same is obvious to me because a little verse has been sent to this column by an aspiring young bard as follows:

'Ba, ba, black sheep have you any wool?
Yes, sir yes, sir three bags full.
One for my master who clipped me nice and tight,
And one for the little boy who washed me oh so white.'

Even if no great amount of midnight oil is burned in the penning of this frivolous but succinct masterpiece, just think how soon another Dylan Thomas or embryo Ben Brock might come to light if only electricity could be got into the darkest corners of Wales.

Come to think of it, how much whiter could a lamb be washed, and how much closer could he be clipped with an electrically driven pressure washer and an electrically driven clipper?

We must look into it.

Welsh Farm News, 26 August 1961

It is my duty to record an interesting, if not hugely funny, little happening from a local show.

The breeder and owner of the sow could not be present at the show because he was attending a wedding. He therefore had someone else to show the sow for him.

The gentleman who showed the sow, and can therefore be referred to as the shower — only make sure you pronounce it right because he is one who shows and not a shower like the RSPCA or soaking of rain — made a very good job of it.

So keen was he that he kept shaking a match-box half-full of matches as the sow was going round the ring. Eventually the judge says to the shower: 'That is a very good idea,' he says, 'to shake the match-box to attract the sow's attention.'

And the shower says: 'Oh, no,' he says, 'It is not to attract the sow's attention,' he says. 'It's to attract your attention.'

The judge gave him the championship for his cheek, and everybody bought drinks all round afterwards on the strength of it.

And the biggest round of all was bought by the breeder and owner who turned up from the wedding, complete with suede shoes and button-hole and smoking a cigar.

And the gentleman who showed the reserve champion said he would have a match-box next time and a good time was had by all. And I know, for I was there.

Welsh Farm News, 21 October 1961

I feel like writing a column for you this week about not much because that is when you haven't anything much about which to write.

As I have told you before on previous occasions, a wise old editor who taught me much in this trade in words said: 'The weather, my boy, is a never failing help in time of trouble. When in doubt,' he said, 'give 'em the weather. For the weather is always topical.'

Now you will notice I sincerely hope and trust that it is a long time indeed since I have to write anything for you about the weather, and you will appreciate from this that you have been getting very good value for your money in being able to read much sound comment on subjects various.

My only point in referring to the weather at this particular moment in time, apart from the fact that there is nothing much else about which to write, is to draw your attention to the great amount of fog which has been hanging about, and is a great traditional custom at this time of year.

Now whilst fog is a condition of the elements which I loathe and despise at all times and in all places, except maybe when I am robbing a bank or some such nefarious business which you do not want to shout from the housetops, it so happens that I loathe and despise fog most of all in London.

I have told you before that London is a big place where you do not go if you have any sense or choice in the matter. But it so happens that you have to go there now and again, especially for such events as the Dairy Show, which is a very great occasion whereunto many people gather from all over the place.

And when I go to London on such occasions it is often my practice which you wot of for me to write a little piece for you about this and that, but chiefly that.

In fact, especially that. And I have never felt the same about London since I was accosted by what you might call one of them and which was a most frightening experience.

It was on one of those occasions when some jollified Scots had hailed me as being next-best-thing to one of their countrymen and seen me best part of the way to the dignified establishment where it had been arranged that I should spend the night.

It was as I peered into the Stygian gloom that one of them loomed up and asked me was I looking. And as I had no ideas about robbing a bank or other such shady or nefarious practice at that particular moment of time I held on to my hat boss and ran as if the old Nick himself was after me in person.

So you will see that the thought of going to London in the fog is most repulsive, and it is why I am very often compared to Columbus, who was a great character in his time, and it is said of him that when he set off he didn't know where he was going, when he got there he didn't know where he was, and when he came back he didn't know where the Hell he'd been.

This is how I always feel when I go to London, only more so when there is dense fog here and there and all about the place. And the only thing I can think of to solve this problem is maybe to borrow the car of a farmer friend, which is a most peculiar vehicle these days which ever way you look at it.

For only recently he is thinking to get this thing fixed up with all mod. cons., which includes getting the trafficator fixed good and proper so that it will work. Well it works all right both ways, but there is one considerable problem.

Somebody has got the wires crossed, which is a very modern expression used by all sorts of people in high office who drop clangers and do not know what they are talking about. And getting wires crossed in a car like this can be most confusing and likewise also embarrassing.

For the way it is working just now is that when he puts the trafficator out to the right, the horn also decides to blow. And this is more confusing than you might think, and not nearly as funny as the loquacious fools in the back would have you believe by their foolish laughter ha-ha.

The idea is, however, that if you keep turning to the left it will work out in the end, so maybe it might be an idea at that to borrow this car, because at least it's something if you can be sure to get back to where you started. And where I started was to say that I felt like writing a column about not much, which is what I have done and what d'you know about that. Maybe you'll be offered something better next week. And maybe you won't.

For as you know I was converted into becoming a teetotaler at the Dairy Show last year — a state of health which wears off in time. And there is a rumour going round that they have now tried using A.I. to cross mules with cows to get milk with a kick in it.

And if you get to drinking stuff like that you never know what might happen to you.

Especially in the fog.

Welsh Farm News, 27 January 1962

Whilst I have always believed that the best place for snow is on a Christmas card, the weather experienced during the recent icy blast brought home once more that every cloud has a silver lining.

This truth manifested itself rather unexpectedly with only three members turning up for the Parish Council meeting. In retrospect, which is a kind of educated way of saying thinking about it the next day, this seems to pass all comprehension.

I say this because the Clerk had received notion of motion regarding the state of the footpaths with a view to having the work done for the improvement of same.

The only logical explanation came out in the local afterwards when one of the quieter ones pointed out that nine times out of ten under such conditions only two would have been daft enough to turn up. But the Council has recently been augmented by a newcomer from suburbia, who was immediately recognised as an enthusiast and got himself co-opted for his trouble.

Not knowing any better, this Charlie turned up to make it three, which the Clerk advised was a quorum, and the only thing he knew of as being next best to a consortium and away they went.

The footpath section had all stayed away for various and doubtlessly valid reasons, but that was so much the worse for them. For the Council as therein constituted got the bit well and truly between their teeth and planned out the whole ding-dong for the remainder of the footpath season.

All the paths as delineated on the County Council map shall now be made fit before the summer.

There is also a minute which ordains that where this work cannot be paid for by the product of a penny rate, the remainder shall be done on a voluntary basis by the members of the footpath section.

The newcomer from suburbia, who wouldn't know any better, supported all this, and the Clerk, who is no more helpful than he ought to be, didn't enlighten him. When the Chairman turned up just before closing time and challenged the Clerk's advice, the latter merely called for another round and said so what, and it would be nice to see all the paths trimmed out anyway.

The Chairman also happens to be a member of the footpath section.

Well, now it is time for me to let you into a secret, which is that I write about the matter in this way because that's the way it is explained to the Chairman. Not surprisingly he is now taking a couple of nights off from watching the telly in order to word a letter to the Clerk instructing him to call a special meeting.

When it takes place a full attendance is guaranteed and, when the minutes are read out, they will learn to their very great surprise that discussion of the question of footpaths is deferred in the absence of the footpath section, and that the only matter dealt with is the complaint that the bulb in the new street lamp has been smashed.

The Clerk pointed out that the light had been placed immediately over the seat where the youngsters do their courting and, on the motion of the newcomer from suburbia, it is agreed that the smashing of the bulb in the new street lamp be accepted as constructive criticism.

A recommendation will accordingly be forwarded to the appropriate authority to the effect that the light be moved.

Welsh Farm News, 24 February 1962

I hope you will agree that I am such a badger as will always listen to good advice, especially when it is given by technical gentlemen who know what they are talking about. The only proviso is that I like them to be able to back up their advice with some good sound argument, if and when the whole thing is not abundantly clear from the word go.

I mention this because I recently receive a visit from one of my favourite advisers, and I grasp the opportunity to put to him a problem which makes me ponder and consider to a very great extent for some time. The problem is about sheep and feeding and management of same. Being a most progressively-minded badger I am always anxious to hot up on the old efficiency lark, and this includes keeping the small baa-lambs going round and round in small paddocks, which cuts down on worm infestation and you can see that I know quite a bit about it.

But the big problem is that, whilst any fool can do this and have the place crawling with sheep in the summer, it is also necessary for working out some sort of workable plan for keeping the ewes through the winter. Which means thinking about things something considerable and having the right food at the right time and in the right place.

So I tell my favourite adviser that we manage to do that this year by having some very nice kale to rush the ewes along smartish during January and February, which is a very good idea calculated to prevent twin-lamb disease as advised by all the best people, especially after keeping the ewes a bit poor during the Autumn.

But I also explain that it seems to cause quite a bit of this old foot trouble which you read about, and he looks very serious and says not only that, but he is against feeding kale to the pregnant animal, and uses one or two long words to back up his point, whilst I try to look as if I understand.

At the outset I put his mind at rest by assuring him that we definitely use ewe-and-lamb nuts, because some of the boys who work for the same firm as he does spend quite a bit of time going round flogging this sort of thing, whilst my favourite adviser spends some time going round flogging good advice.

And it is very good advice indeed to tell a farmer to feed the ewe well prior to lambing, and if you have any sense of loyalty at all, obviously you will buy the nuts which are made by the firm which employs him to go round giving good advice, and let me state that I have no objection to this not nohow.

So then we get round to talking about the wild months of January and February, and we agree that, although ryegrass is a food most succulent, January and February are months when there is a good chance of having snow if you are going to have any at all.

That brings us back to the kale, but I say in any case that I decide long ago that kale is out as far as I am concerned, except as a catch crop, and although I base my arguments on my experience with cows, the same thing will apply for sheep or anything else which has to eat off this expensive crop.

So my favourite adviser pushes back his hat and lights up his pipe, which gives him much time to think, and then he looks straight at me and asks me do I ever think about mangolds. And I have much pleasure to tell him yes, that in my time I grow many mangel-wurzels and have great faith in them as a food most juicy and nutritious for all manner of livestock in due season, they are certainly to be commended.

But I go on to explain that I am a lazy badger and that growing mangolds sounds very much to me like hard work. I also hasten to add that I am likewise a very poor badger and do not think I will ever have the sort of money necessary to pay somebody else to do all this work for me.

So then we have some chit-chat on the question of precision drilling and selective weed-killers and this and that, but I am still not entirely convinced as a result of which we proceed to have some talk on the relative yields which can be expected under certain varying conditions.

This leads to a remarkable statement on the part of my adviser who says that on the banks of the Jordan it is very fertile and therefore capable of growing very heavy crops. What is more, Palestine is the only place where he ever sees a Jew working on the land in all his life, and I say indeed it must be very fertile. But I also say that the only time I ever look over Jordan what do I see but a band of angels coming after me for to carry me home.

The only thing is, I hope and trust you will not advise me to go back to growing mangolds. In fact I think I will rather go to the Jordan and give myself up to the angels than suffer such a death and thank you for nothing.

Welsh Farm News, 6 October 1962

If this ever sees the light of day you will know that all is well, more or less, even if it is only just, because at one time it looks as if I will never be writing a column for you ever again.

You will remember that the last time I write a little piece for you I am generally just a little bit fed up with one and all, and therefore I decide to take a few days to get in some heavy work on the old peace and quiet lark, because I am a great believer in this at all times as being a very good cure for many ailments including being run down, tired, overworked and other such distressing maladies.

That is why I explain to you I am going away to this island where I can watch the seals and that, and I leave in such great haste that I have no time to write a little piece for you before I go. What is more, I cannot even think what there is for me to write about. The well is dry. I am, as the saying goes, bereft of reason and am without inspiration in any shape or form.

However, I do not let this worry me unduly because I am a great believer in a spot of peace and quiet to rectify such matters, and I decide I will maybe write a little piece for you whilst I am on this island in my own good time and do not rush these matters.

Anyway everything goes all right, and we reach this island in considerable safety, but with not much to spare as it is somewhat rough at the time. I would also ask you to take note of this use of the first person pronoun in the plural as you might say because I am not alone.

In fact we are very much in the plural. There is one character who has a slipped disc and is in very poor shape generally, and I cannot see a very large amount of peace and quiet putting him right. He also has a little bottle from which he has to put drops into his eyes every few hours, and in addition to this he has many cameras and accompanying impedimenta in order to take pictures of the seals and the peace and the quiet and all this and that.

There is also one small badger very much present and correct because he wishes to learn about these matters, and in any case he thinks that life on an island must be fun. That's a laugh that is. I'll tell you. That's a laugh.

Naturally Mrs Brock will not be very happy to allow this small badger to travel alone with a parent in search of peace and quiet and such characters as go about the place with cameras and slipped discs, putting drops in their eyes. It is therefore very easy to persuade Mrs Brock that she will very much enjoy such a quiet week-end as that of which I am now about to speak.

Well, everything goes along very nicely, and there is much peace and quiet everywhere, and fresh air very sweet and wholesome all about the place, and the sun shining in spite of the fact that it is blowing very hard. So the first morning we are here I go with this character and the small badger to take some of these pictures of all these seals and their pups.

We use this rope to get down the steep track down this cliff and end up on a pebbly beach with the wild waves pounding and seals everywhere to be seen. Then we go into a big dark cave and I am carrying the camera for this other character as he is in great trouble on these pebbles on account of his slipped disc.

Once we are inside the cave I climb up on a big boulder, which is very greasy on account of the sea and darkness and all that, and immediately fall lens over shutter and plunge about ten thousand feet onto my back. It is very painful.

Even so this other character thinks it is all highly amusing and a great diversion from thinking about his slipped disc, and he speaks as follows: 'It is a great shame,' he says, 'that I do not have a camera ready.' He says, 'I think it will be great fun ha-ha to take a picture of you in such a position.' But it is some time before he can say all this because of his great amusement.

Anyway we manage to get back up the cliff and back to the farmhouse for dinner and, apart from the head boss man of this place and his family, there are also two other characters, male and female, who just arrive in search of peace and quiet and likewise also some pictures, and it is in every way a very welcome and enjoyable meal and, like the boy scout's pastry, well cooked.

The only thing that spoils the meal for me is the great lack of manners of all the other characters round the table, including my own nearest and dearest, because they all take great delight in making mock of affliction, and they are far more amused by the description of my fall as given by the fool with the slipped disc than they are sympathetic on account of my own great suffering.

I explain that I have in fact broken a finger in this fall, so they say how can I now write my column for the newspaper, so that I then point out I have only broken the finger in my left hand which they agree is not at all important as it will not prevent me writing my column.

Even so, it is necessary for me to go to bed for what is known as a nap, and I think that by the time I wake up I will maybe have some inspiration to write a column for you. So I do this, and in spite of the fact that there is a great gale blowing I go to sleep. Very soon, however, I am awakened by a great deal of shouting from the beach below.

It is the head boss man of this island and he is in a great state of agitation, so I grab some shoes and a large mackintosh because it is now raining very furious and I dash to help him. Unfortunately, on the greasy bank my feet go from under me, and I suffer another great fall in exactly the same place including my arm and my elbow.

But there is no time to bother about this, because the boat is being pounded on the rocks by the great waves and it is most distressing. So the head boss man says I must go with him in the boat, and as I am such a simple soul who should not be allowed out without his mamma, and as I cannot think of any quick excuse like having a wife and family, until it is too late, I jump into the boat and fall on the same elbow and arm again.

We get the engine going and get her off the rocks, and we manage to get out to the mooring where there are great chains and all this and that fastened to a buoy for keeping a boat at such times as this. But once we are there we find we cannot get back against the wind in a rowing boat because the wind is blowing about a thousand miles an hour.

The head boss man says to me, 'You cannot swim can you?' So I look at him very hurt and say, 'Do you not hear that in my time I am a very great swimmer with medals and certificates and all that and, in fact, I cleave through the water like an arrow. But that is many years ago,' I say, 'and I do not think I will do very much cleaving like an arrow in my present state of health.'

'Never mind,' says the head boss man. 'It is like riding a bicycle. Once you learn how to do it you never forget it. Even so,' he says, 'I think we will now put lifejackets on.'

So we do this, and I cannot help thinking that if we do land up in the drink the seals will be greatly perplexed at what we are supposed to be doing, especially in these outfits.

In fact at this time they are dodging all round in the sea and looking at us most surprised, and they are no doubt thinking that human beings are very odd creatures, but they do not understand about peace and quiet and such matters.

Then the head boss man says, 'Do you think you now have enough to write about in your column?' and I say, 'Yes, if you will please take me back to the island or anywhere out of this mayhem I will now be pleased to make an immediate start on the writing.'

I also say that if it was half as bad as this at the time they tried to cross the dark and stormy waters, then Lord Ulin's daughter and the Chief of Ulva's Isle must have been a couple of nut cases. By this time it is getting dark as well as raining and blowing, but there is a great amount of white everywhere, which is the foam and the spray of the waves which are pounding us every which way. The rowing boat has also filled with water and gone to the bottom and I do not at this time give much for my chances of ever writing a column for you again.

As we see the oars of the dinghy wash away in the gloom I understand the meaning of the expression, 'up the creek without a paddle.'

The head boss man says the boat weighs a couple of tons, but he does not take into account that she is bows under and has shipped about ninety-five tons of water. However, it is now high tide so we get the engine going again and make one last desperate run for it against the wind and the tide.

The next thing I know I am up on the jetty with a rope in my hand and I have landed on the same elbow and arm again, but there is no time for me to dwell on such matters as the head boss man is shouting his head off for me to pull on the rope like hallelujah-glory-be, and he is not taking the ninety-five tons of water into account.

Immediately, the character with a slipped disc, followed by the other characters male and female, loom up out of the darkness and we get the ropes onto a big winch and there is much turning and heaving as is both customary and necessary at such times, not to mention a great deal of shouting and such like.

In the middle of it, something goes wrong and the winch handle swings round and cops me a fourpenny on the same arm and elbow, which makes me see about twenty seven thousand stars of different colours, shapes and sizes. It is evident by this time that I will finish up with nothing less than gangrene, but I am so wet and cold that I do not let it bother me. There is sea water running out through my earholes, and my eyes are red and raw from the salt water.

It is well after midnight before we know that the boat is safe, and then I drink four times as much rum as anyone else, because it is recognised that I am on the delicate side, and they all assure me it is a certain antidote against gangrene.

That is about all there is to the story, except to state that the other character on the winch is the one with the slipped disc. When he manages eventually to straighten up he finds that his slipped disc is greatly improved. In fact I think he will now be fit to carry his own cameras.

What is more he is now open to receive offers for his bottle of eyedrops because all the salt water from the waves breaking over him has put him as good as new, and his eyes are perfect again and obviously very healthy. The salt water is very healing.

Furthermore I have all the inspiration I need for a column thank you very much, and this explains why I am such a great believer in all this peace and quiet as a certain cure for complaints various.

Welsh Farm News, 22 December 1962

The time of year is upon us when it behoves one and all to wish each other ye Merrie Christmas with tender thoughts and hearty greetings, which is why I decide to explain to you some more about efficiency in case you have not yet reached a proper understanding of this attribute most commendable.

Furthermore it is also incumbent on me to explain that I pen these unhappy lines immediately upon my return from London and Smithfield and the soul-destroying Smog.

Sufficient has already been written on this subject, however, to render it unnecessary for me to prolong the agony. In fact there is neither the desire nor the intention on my part so to do. But speak to you of my experiences on the last day I must. It behoves me.

Intoxicated by the sight of so much tinsel and bright lights and a large number of whatever is plural for Father Christmas here and there and everywhere else as soon as the fog had cleared, the thought occurred to me that I would do what is popularly known as some Christmas shopping, and which in my own case is confined to two purchases. I do not believe in trespassing upon the Home Secretary's domain.

Furthermore, long years of married life, and purchases made more in hope than in good taste, have brought with them an increasing measure of sympathy and understanding for the faithful dog who looks in vain for the kind word of reward from its master. That is why I am kind to dogs, and years ago learned to play it safe and settle for stockings. Unimaginative and unromantic maybe, but old age does not come by itself.

If there is any young married man seeking guidance from these utterances, I would hasten to add, 'Don't just buy one pair, you nit. Because once one stocking has laddered, the other is useless. You buy two pairs of the same shade. This is a modified version of increasing efficiency, and you can write it all down to experience. What is more, if you really want to get into the good books, you needn't stop at two pairs.'

Thus it came about that I effected my first purchase at a very high-class-looking establishment, and there is a funny little story pertaining to this, but I do not wish to speak of such frivolous matters just at the moment.

The other purchase was to be for one small badger and, being ever mindful of the need to set small feet on the right road, I decided to buy him a pair of football stockings. He already has the ball and the boots and the shorts and the jersey, so that you will see that his religious education is being well taken care of.

The thought also occurred in passing that, not having smoked for over twelve years, and if I effected certain economies for the next twelve months, I might possibly be able to mortgage my future to the extent of a long-playing operatic record for my own indulgence.

Chiefly, however, with the small rugby stockings in mind, I entered one of these mighty emporiums at which the mind boggles, and made straight for the gaudy and prefabricated Mecca of the village idiot whereon was writ, bold and clear, the magic word 'Information', and wherein reposed, most elegantly groomed and manicured, two female characters whose job I presumed, quite reasonably I thought, would be to answer sympathetically the queries of those who are of an enquiring turn of mind.

I had neither qualm, misgiving, nor hesitation, therefore, in asking the first one who deigned to turn her head in my direction whether she could be so kind as to direct me to the sports department. Whereupon she asked me what I wanted, so I told her, and she says they just do not sell anything like that at all.

So I say well thank you very much and in that case can she tell me where their music department is. And she looks at me in a most supercilious manner and says, 'We haven't one of those either. You are unlucky this morning, aren't you?'

I believe repartee is generally reckoned to be the smart answer you think of ten minutes too late. That's what usually happens to me anyway. But I have my moments, and I like to think that this was one of them. For, like the B.A. from Aberystwyth, quick as a flash the answer came, and witty with it. I said, 'No indeed, sweetheart. You're unlucky. I've got some money to spend, and you've got the rent to find. Good morning each.'

Once again out in the maelstrom of cavorting taxi-cabs and seething humanity I was fortunate enough to heave-to alongside a large policeman of measured gait and benign visage and he, having heard me out patiently, and doubtlessly thinking he was being helpful, directed me to the mightiest of all the mighty emporiums in this mighty city which was situated no more than the length of a couple of good fields and a burgage from where we stood.

Of the remainder of my expedition it would be possible to write at great length, but I shall be as brief as possible. Apart from the fact that I have no wish to weary you, neither do I wish to revive the sort of memories which are apt to make ordinary mortals wake up screaming in the night.

The painted creation on Information knew immediately where the sports department was – fourth floor. Thus I set out via a series of escalators, and again I will not weary you with details of shopping baskets, sharp-ended umbrellas, recalcitrant small children in harnesses and on leads over which big badgers are liable to trip without warning, and which collectively comprised the gauntlet it was apparently necessary to run in order to reach the fourth floor.

Loudspeakers at strategic points up and down the

escalators, and young gentlemen in striped trousers at both ends, enjoined the throng to keep moving. They had a hope and all, mate.

Eventually, however, the nightmare ordeal was over and I found myself on the fourth floor. As far as I could make out it was chiefly cafés and restaurants and such.

So I addressed myself to a commissionaire type of gentleman, who had a mountain of gold braid, a peaked cap and what not, and also, so it transpired, had been supplied with a kind of tourist guide, who assured me that there was nothing faintly resembling a sports department on that floor, and said, after prolonged reference to his *multum-in-parvo*, that I would find it on the third floor down below – down the escalator.

It turned out it was right at the far end of the building, but I arrived there at last and eventually managed to button-hole a large, well-fed and morning-suited gentleman who said, 'Not a hope, old chap. Nothing less than size eight. You haven't got a hope. Why not try in children's wear? Same floor as this, far end of the building.'

The best the lady there could offer me was a pair of small girl's hockey stockings. When I explained that we had never been blessed with a small girl badger but only a small boy badger, she said, 'Why not try the boys' wear department?' So I says, 'Then what is this?' And she looks at me as if I'm the only half-wit they have there, and she says, 'This is the girls' wear department.'

No doubt that was why they had small girls' hockey stockings, or maybe it was just coincidence. So, summoning up my last failing reserves of politeness, I asked her then, please, where was the boys' wear department. And she said – well, what do you think she said? – she said, 'Next floor down, other end.'

Then they talk to farmers about efficiency and work study.

If nothing else it has at least provided me with an excuse to write this deathless prose for you, but I find little else to commend their carryings-on. At passing the buck these establishments are adept. Getting what you want has become an occupational hazard.

For example, at this year's BOCM luncheon at a well-known hostelry in Park Lane, which was given to some of their friends in conjunction with their National Milk Yield Competition, I completely failed to obtain a glass of milk. It's one thing to produce milk, but quite another to try to get a glass of it where the population of waiters is measured by the square yard.

At one time in years gone by there was a jug of milk on every table, but hardly anybody drank it. So now you can't get it because it seems it must be all or nothing, and those who exhort us to produce more milk would not appear to regard it as also being their function to promote the demand for it.

It was with something of these thoughts in mind that I assailed the last bastion in my quest for a pair of small rugby stockings. They did not appear to be unduly hard-pressed in the boys' wear department. Maybe their customers are not all as enterprising and determined as I am.

A pleasant young gentleman, in standard morning suit, came up to me, half-bowed most politely, and said, 'Can I help you, sir?'

I regret to say, I said, 'If you can, you're the first so-and-so I've met in this place this morning who can.' Except that I didn't say so-and-so, and I'll give you two guesses what I did say, and if you can't guess then, well you must be a more stupid lot of so-and-so's than I thought you were.

'Now, now, sir,' says he, with a merry twinkle in his eye, 'What's the trouble?'

So I told him, and before you could say 'wheel and take' there they were in red and white stripes, laid out

63

before my eyes. And all at once the years slipped away, and once again I was very young.Which also explains something about Christmas, for surely this is a very special time for the little ones.

---

12 July 1956

In father's footsteps

The old bull called his three young sons together and explained to them that they were about to go out into the world and plough their own furrow.

What, then, did they want to be?

"Well, for my part, father," said the first young bull, "I'd like to be a bull in a china shop."

"H'm. Yes. Not a bad plan at all" says the old bull. "I've never tried it myself, but I imagine a chap could have a lot of fun at that. And what about you, my boy?" addressing the second one.

"Well, father, if it's all the same to you I'd like to go on the Stock Exchange."

"Not a bad plan, son. No doubt you'll find it very interesting."

Then, turning a doubtful eye on the third youngster, "How about you, fellah?"

"Aw, gee pop. I ain't got no high-falutin' ideas. I just wanna follow in your footsteps an' be a cowboy."

Welsh Farm News, 21 August 1963

'What's in a name? That which we call a rose by any other name would smell as sweet.'

Something like that was what Shakespeare said, if I remember correctly, and he seemed to know about such matters.

I am prompted to these reflections by the news that 'Miss England' has just been adjudged runner-up out in California in a contest to decide who should be 'Miss International Beauty of 1963.'

By all accounts Miss England seems to have what it takes, including dimensions of 36-23-36, and I am reliably informed that these are very good dimensions indeed.

The name of this young lady in real life escapes me for the moment, but it seems that, before she changes it to whatever she is, she is just plain Miss Hickingbotham, and, me being me, I wouldn't mind betting that, somewhere along the line before that, it is, in any case, changed from just plain Hickingbottom.

Anyway she decides to change from being Miss Hickingbotham because the name doesn't sound very elegant, and I don't see how anybody can argue with her on that score. Apparently she receives a prize out of all this of £1,400 and is quoted as saying that she doesn't know what she is going to do with the money.

I suppose she could buy a new tractor and pick-up baler but, come to think of it, the season is getting a bit advanced for that sort of thing and it's cheaper to get the harvesting done by contract.

In any case I think that her thoughts do not run on these lines because her ambition is to become a top model.

This is a very classy profession by all account, and I understand that the models here and there and round and about have recently been getting rather cross because of the frequency with which the newspapers refer to a certain Miss Christine Keeler* as a model. Apparently the real classy models do not think much of this at all, because maybe she is not a very good model.

When it becomes known that Miss Keeler is commissioned to write some pieces about her boudoir memoirs the models seem to think that they are getting their own back by referring to Miss Keeler as the well-known journalist. I think this surely must prove something, but I can't for the life of me imagine what it is, except that the models obviously have a sense of humour very much after my own heart.

I hope Miss Hickingbotham achieves her ambition no matter what they call her. For my own part I am called all sorts of names in my time, but I never let it bother me as I always adopt Missus Reilly's philosophy that they can call me what the devil they like as long as they don't call me early in the morning.

In any case Miss Hickingbotham does at least change her name of her own volition, as distinct from having some other name thrust upon her in the manner of thousands of characters who have nick-names given to them, subsequently to go through life known by nothing else.

Take Dai What'll-You-Bet, for instance. At the slightest sign of argument or difference of opinion in any shape, manner or form, Dai will immediately say 'What'll-you-bet?'

The whole business finally culminates when one of his workmates is killed, and it is left to Dai to go and break the news to his wife, because he is the senior man on the job and also kind and tactful at all times.

So Dai goes round and knocks on the door and, to the lady who answers, Dai says, 'Are you Billy Jones's widow?'

'I'm Billy Jones's wife,' she says, and Dai says, 'What'll you bet?'

The list is never ending, and maybe you are wondering what all this has to do with farming, and for that matter I am beginning to think the same thing myself. But some of you very often say to me how is it possible to go on churning out stuff week after week, and I explain that sometimes it is a bit of a problem at that.

And between you and me, and I do hope you will not let on to anybody about this, it so happens that this is one of those weeks, and the sands of time are running out, and somebody is likely to say to me what about my column, or copy as it is called, and I can only say yes indeed what about it.

Then all of a sudden up pops this bit of news about Miss Hickingbotham, and I think to myself this is surely a most suitable subject on which to discourse, because most of the County Federations of Young Farmers' Clubs now seem to hold their County Rallies and chose their Rally Queens for the season.

So far there does not seem to be a Miss Hickingbotham in the list. Furthermore I am of the opinion that if one of them is born Miss Hickingbotham, then Hickingbotham she will remain until some honest young farmer changes it for her.

And if you feel disposed to say that you think I am talking great foolishness, then I can only say to you, 'What'll you bet?'

---

* Christine Keeler did start off as a model, which she hoped to make her vocation, but she became 'a lady of easy virtue', involved in high society and political intrigue beyond her understanding, which led to the downfall of the politician John Profumo. Other models objected to newspapers referring to her as a 'model', and when articles then began to appear under her name, and referring to her as a model, the models began to hit back by referring to her as 'a well-known journalist'. She was certainly well-known, if not for her journalism.

Welsh Farm News, 31 August 1963

'Talking Points'

Please don't think I am one of those who would advocate a return of the rabbit, but passing a railway truck the other day I was interested to see cardboard cartons labelled 'Skinned Australian rabbit.'

I am assured that wild rabbits at the present time are meeting with a good trade and I couldn't help thinking that, at the price milk has been lately, it wouldn't have done any harm to have a few hundred rabbits to catch and sell. After all, the breeding and housing costs are nil and there is only the food they eat to offset against the return they bring.

Not that I'm in favour of rabbits as I have said — but it makes you think. Eight rabbits they say equals one sheep and I suppose 16 or 20 rabbits equals one cow.

Which shows the highest profit, leaving aside all thoughts of farming tradition and good husbandry?

[Name and address withheld.]

Welsh Farm News, 14 September 1963

Notwithstanding anything expressed or implied in the many thousands of words I have previously written on the subject of rabbits, clearance of same and damage by ditto, I wish to make it perfectly clear that I neither agree nor disagree with the recent comment on the subject in *Talking Points,* and I also agree and disagree.

This is due to the Irish blood in me manifesting itself again. I do not know the writer or writers, singular or plural, of *Talking Points* and therefore I am quite sure that he, she or they will not take any offence whatsoever about my writing in this vein. Because I, too, find the rabbit to be very tasty and very sweet, likewise also a dish most tender and succulent at many seasons of the year.

I also think it is a good idea if you have a rabbit to sell, and in fact I am all in favour of having anything to sell because times are cruel hard, friends. There is, however, a great danger in regarding the rabbits as something for nothing as it were, because they are the most costly brutes anyone could ever produce on a free-range system.

There are two reasons why the sale of rabbits cannot be compared with the sale of milk or beef or lamb. To start with, the price per pound you get for your rabbit is considerably less than the price per pound you get for your beef or lamb. Or, to include milk in the reckoning, and to reduce the problem to present day parlance, your output per acre is so reduced that your margin is completely minimised. And that's a hell of an awful old complaint.

The other vital point is the question of the food they eat, and that is where reasoning can sometimes go way off beam. Because, in the final reckoning, it is not merely off-setting the food they eat against the return they bring. If it were only the food they eat which had to be reckoned up against them there wouldn't be much argument, and I'm a great believer in the principle of live and let live, or at any rate as far as it is possible.

In fact sometimes of an evening when I am enjoying an all too rare spell of comfort and relaxation with my feet up in front of the fire after another day of fearful toil, a moth will zoom down out of the nethermost darkness behind the goggle-box, and Mrs Brock will say for me to do something about it most immediate.

And I must admit that at such times I am apt to say does it really matter and the world is plenty big enough for him and me. And although this argument maybe doesn't hold much water, it is always worth a try if it enables you to keep your feet up in front of the fire without having to jump about all over the place after another day of fearful toil, although I am not often allowed to get away with it.

The argument of live and let live, however, does not hold good in the case of the little bunny rabbits because of the fearful amount of damage they do. If a price anything like their real cost to the farmer could be placed on the rabbits then it would be found that they are the most expensively produced commodity anybody could ever wish to avoid producing.

Nor is this the sum total of the bill, because on top of the damage done to growing crops there is the cost of housing the brutes, as any farmer can testify who has seen them tear down hedge banks which were made at a time when men knew how to do such a job of work, and when to pay a man to do such a job didn't automatically lead to bankruptcy.

Indeed if we now had the plague of rabbits which we had before the coming of myxomatosis I am pretty sure that many farmers could not survive with the margin on livestock products produced from grass reduced to what it is. And if they were to be enabled to stay in business under such conditions, then the price of food would have to go up quite a bit from what it is at present.

Therefore, every farmer in his right mind knows that rabbits have to be kept down, and that is where we come to the big talking point.

On principle, I endeavour to be agin the Government in general and the Min. of Ag. and Fish in particular, and generally speaking this is no great difficulty. But I am bound to admit that the Government made by far and away the greatest single contribution to rabbit clearance by outlawing the gin trap.

I have previously explained why it is that the gin trap only increases the rabbit population, and if anybody cannot understand that by now they are truly beyond hope. But that doesn't matter because the gin trap has been made illegal, and it only remains for me to say that anybody adopting the gin trap as the *modus operandi* for tackling the rabbit problem ought to be locked up.

It is now just on ten years since we were troubled by the rabbit, and many enthusiastic types thought that the time was opportune to make an almighty and all-out effort to wipe the rabbit off the face of our fair and pleasant land. They found in the fullness of time, however, that this couldn't be done not nohow.

Therefore we have found that we still have some rabbits here and there, and we have to learn to live with them whilst trying to live without them. And I have always reckoned that by using a lamp and a good dog by night, and a ferret by day, the rabbits that survive won't trouble anybody very much.

No doubt the best way to tackle this is by means of a rabbit clearance society, but if your society happens to be no more use than the one which operates in this area there is no need for you to lose any sleep about it, because with a rabbit being in good demand there is no trouble in getting some of the types who specialise in such matters in their spare time to run the lurcher round the field one night with the lamp.

Such types will also dig for hours after a ferret until they're in a lather of sweat, but somehow always find digging the garden much more of a burden, and I have to admit that I come into this category when it comes to digging the garden.

I think it is therefore a good thing that rabbits are in such demand and that no-one has taken any notice of all the congenital idiots who have talked about outlawing the sale of rabbits and burying them instead of eating them.

Brambles aren't exactly the hallmark of good husbandry, but that doesn't prevent my being very partial to a blackberry tart, and Mrs Brock is such an excellent cook, with such a beautifully light hand when it comes to making pastry, that it's no wonder I would prefer to keep my feet up in front of the fire of an evening rather than cavort about the kitchen in pursuit of zooming moths after another day of fearful toil.

I do not go along with the balance of nature outfit, who very often don't know what they're talking about, on the question of rabbits, because rabbits are not indigenous to these islands and we could very well do without them. But I very much doubt whether we shall see the end of them in our time.

Therefore we learn to live in spite of them, keep them down most stringently by proper methods of control, which doesn't mean trapping or gassing, and most definitely enjoy every tasty succulent morsel most sweet and tender that comes our way.

Fortunately, as yet, if anybody wishes to buy such a tasty morsel off you for hard cash there's no law against selling it.

Welsh Farm News, 21 September 1963

A couple of years ago I told you that we had had our road beautifully tarred. I also had my little say about the idiots who ordain that these things shall come to pass and are known as Surveyors, who answer, in theory, to bigger idiots known as County Councillors who fill in many claim forms for expenses.

During the two years since then the most excellent gentleman whose task in life it is to attend to the ditches has rarely been able to do so, because he has constantly been taken away from his 'length' to work with a gang.

That being so the ditches have mostly been bunged up with growth, and the water has therefore been running down all over the road.

It is not done to complain of such matters because we would be asked did we not know we were well off to have our road tarred twice in two years.

Years ago I worked out a simple philosophy that all Councillors are fools. Half of them have no brains and are therefore fools. The other half have brains and are therefore bigger fools for wasting their time with the half who haven't. Therefore all Councillors are fools.

The joke is that you can propound this theory to Councillors, and they will take no offence. In fact they will laugh hearty and agree with you, because they are satisfied that they are in the half with all the brains.

That must be the half responsible for allowing idiot Surveyors to take roadmen off their 'length' to work in gangs.

So help me!

Welsh Farm News, 5 October 1963

As some of you will know from the occasional reference in this column it is a source of great comfort to me from time to time to be able to get away to the islands off the coast of West Wales.

This is an exercise which doeth great good by virtue of the fact that there is much walking to be done, and it is also possible to sleep for hours on end because there is no telephone in such remote places. It is also possible to forget all manner of troubles and let the rest of the world go by. In fact it is a great life for anyone who likes to get away from it all.

At one time, as some of you may remember, it is a great idea with me to go to Skomer which is altogether an island most enchanting and very restful. Then, however, sad to relate and as some of you may also remember, this same paradise is acquired by for the nation by the nation in the form of the Nature Conservancy and the rot sets in.

It is leased to a local outfit, which is now known as the West Wales Naturalists Trust, and thereafter descend the hordes of bird-ringers and like tormentors. Much of this sort of thing is strictly the old phonus bolonus.

I also know from what some of you say to me from time to time, and from the letters which sometimes arrive, but which are unfortunately not fit to be printed, that you remember my writing about the joyful experiment of crossing Welsh mountain ewes and Soay ewes. And, notwithstanding anything which the Denning Report* fails to disclose, even in these uncertain times we know enough of the habits of the lascivious bumble-bee on the pollenizing prowl for an unsuspecting virgin rose to know that any sort of ewes don't not mate with no other sort of ewes not nohow.

Then there is also the scandal of some of these Soay

sheep being left on an eighteen acre rock out in the ocean all through a burning drought without food or water, and when they are picked up dead in the winter the head boss character palms off the more humane members by saying they have been struck by lightning. Now I don't know why it is but whenever mention is made of this incident I always think of the character with the talking jay.

It happens many years ago and this character sees an advertisement in a magazine about another character with a Yorkshire canary who wishes to exchange it for a talking jay. Maybe when you hear the story you will think that he does not have any Yorkshire canary at all but just wants a talking jay on the cheap.

Anyway after they exchange letters it is agreed that they should put their respective birds on the respective morning trains, one from the local station and one from Paddington. Well, this character puts his talking jay on the first train in the morning from the local station, but when he goes back to meet the down train in the evening there is no Yorkshire canary. Letters to the character with the Yorkshire canary elicit no reply. So the character now without the talking jay has what he thinks is a bright idea and writes to Scotland Yard.

It turns out that this London character has quite a record at that. But no doubt the police put a bit of a scare into him because he writes to the character who is now without the talking jay explaining that, as he is on his way to Paddington, the Yorkshire canary drops dead off the perch. And the character now without the talking jay, by way of one last despairing shot, immediately sends back an open postcard saying, 'Thou should'st have been on the bloody perch, not the canary.' Now I'd hate you to think from all this that I would wish to see anybody being struck by lightning, not even if they are such characters as will leave little

Soay sheep on an eighteen acre rock out in the ocean all through a burning drought without food and water. But if they are ever out there in such conditions they will know whether the Soay sheep could survive long enough for the lightning to catch up with them because they are much quicker than lightning. There are also other diabolical happenings which are of concern. Once upon a time I write for you about the heathen practice of ringing seals. Now that Skomer has been dedicated to the nation as 'a place where seals and seabirds can live in peace for ever', the ritual has been changed somewhat and the current idea seems to be that the metal tags are not very successful anyway, so they brand the baby seals with red hot irons heated by a portable liquid gas apparatus.

All this in spite of their own admission that baby seals are extremely vulnerable to sepsis during their first three weeks of life. This business of the seals and ringing of same is also much under discussion, because some of the types who go fishing in the rivers get very cross about the seals sometimes.

They say the seals are skulking about round the estuaries and catching the salmon and preventing the salmon from going up the rivers to indulge in such practices as you read about with the birds and the bees and that. And they say that these seals ought to be shot and generally destroyed and kept down and controlled.

But the naturalists don't like this idea, because then there will be fewer seals to torment by putting rings on and stabbing red hot branding irons on them, all of which is most confusing. And the character in charge of the fishing who has to report to the Rivers Board on the predatory habit of these seals is a character by the name of Roscoe Howells which is more confusing still. I have never met or set eyes on this Roscoe Howells character and know nothing at all about him, except that he is in no way connected with the Roscoe Howells character who writes for this paper. So that you can see that what with all the confusion and ringing and phonus bolonus and all this and that and one thing and another generally there is quite a bit from which to get away.

And in fact instead of going to Skomer to get away from it all the idea is now to get away from such things as are happening on Skomer. So last week when I have to go to London I suggest to Mrs. Brock that she should come with me for a few days and that we should take the small badger with us on the premise that, like Albert Ramsbottom, 'a trip to Metrollopse might broaden the little lad's mind.'

Some of you sometimes say about the happenings which I recount in this column that maybe I am stretching it a bit, but I give you my word that the most I ever do is give my own version of how things happen. And I give you my word that what I tell you now is perfectly true.

We take our lives in our hands and go on the pedestrian crossings. We travel on the underground and up and down the moving staircases. We look at old Nelson on his column and feed the pigeons. Eventually, out of sheer fatigue and to rest my aching feet, I suggest an hour's session in the News Theatre. There are cartoons and comical items.

And would you believe it, there am I resting quietly and minding my own business when on comes a film about Skomer, and this is the most comical item of the lot, or will be if it isn't for the fact that it makes me want to vomit. The photography is good, but never in my life outside of the annual general meetings of the West Wales Naturalists Trust, do I ever have to listen to such complete and utter nonsense as is contained in the commentary.

There, in the bowels of the earth beneath the great City with its teeming millions, away from it all, I suffer it all over again. Rings and nets and weighing and the old phonus bolonus as large as life. The name of the effort, as far as I remember, is *Looking at Life*, or some such misleading euphemism. And there is the one badger in the world, who possibly forgets more about Skomer than the whole boiling of quasi-naturalists will ever know, called upon to suffer in impotent silence.

Safe returned I am going through the post and a glance through *Nature in Wales*, the official publication which recounts these goings on, seems to suggest that a sporadic visit to Skomer is paid during January last. And it is faithfully reported that wrens have deserted the island except for ten which were dead.

And dead wrens can't fly so they cannot get away from it all. And I hope you will think yourselves lucky that bird-ringing and weighing and the keenest possible observation combine to establish that dead birds can't fly whether they be wrens or Yorkshire canaries.

I'm just going down to our wood to get away from it all.

---

* The Denning Report was the report of Lord Denning into the Christine Keeler affair, which was generally acknowledged, particularly as time went by and more facts emerged, to be a travesty of the truth.

Welsh Farm News, 2 November 1963

After many thousands of words of experience in the business it is now well-known to me that you are always very interested to hear how things have gone when it has been necessary for me to go away from home, especially if going away from home has involved going as far as London for such matters as the Dairy Show.

London is a big place, likewise also a very wicked place, or so they tell me, but I wouldn't know for sure to be able to speak with any authority on such matters. Certainly large numbers of people seem to be very anxious to go there, and I don't suppose they are all intent on being wicked. In fact some of them are parsons and chapel deacons and such characters who wouldn't do any harm to anybody.

But when you come to take them altogether, what with those who wish to be wicked, as well as the parsons and chapel deacons who wouldn't do any harm to anybody, and add to that number all the miscellaneous badgers who wish to go to the Dairy Show and the Motor show, as well as to see England show the Rest of the World how to play football, you will understand it is indeed a very great number of people to be in one place all at the same time.

It came as no surprise, therefore, when I received a postcard from the decorous establishment where it is my wont to stay for my infrequent visits to the big City for such events as the Dairy Show, regretting that on this occasion they would be unable to avail themselves of the privilege of attending to my meagre requirements, but intimating that they would consider it an honour to be permitted to arrange for me to stay at some other hostelry nearby. I accepted their kind offer.

Anybody but a complete idiot would have known better. Obviously they are not going to put anybody anywhere that's any good. They want to make sure you will come crawling back in gratitude the next time. I can only assume this must be their line of reasoning. How else to explain it? What have I ever done to be subjected to such misery?

Once inside this penitentiary I knew I was doomed. With an instinct born of long years of bitter experience I recognised that it would be worse than useless to waste time in trying to set the joint to rights. Life is too short. The position was obviously as without hope as the ancient and jaded characters, immediately identifiable as residents, who came scuttling in to claw for the miserable portions eked out in the name of breakfast.

Breakfast, to your true countryman, is a meal to be thought about, to be sat down to, savoured and enjoyed. In this case it was a choice between grilled kipper and eggs various.

There was a lift of ancient vintage and creaking mechanism to be self-operated by anyone foolhardy enough to trust to its swaying spasms. As often as not the decision resolved itself because the last fool to have used it hadn't shut the gate, so that it was impossible to summon it from by there to by here.

The first night I didn't sleep at all, and this is not surprising because the traffic thundered by beneath my window with a reverberating regularity that rendered any hope of sleep completely impossible. The weariness thus engendered, followed by a hard day, would normally have ensured a deeper degree of sleep on the second night in spite of the worst the traffic could do.

At something just before midnight I crawled into bed, weary unto limb and mind, and in sore need of the healing that cometh with slumber. At exactly midnight, however, some gentlemen arrived in the street below to mend the road. They were accompanied by a pneumatic drill. And the pneumatic drill was driven by a motor.

I suppose the drill must have been the worst, because when the drill wasn't working you could hear the motor. But there wasn't a great deal to choose between them. Large lumps of cotton wool stuffed into my ears enabled me to retain my sanity, but I won't put it no higher as they say. The gentlemen with the pneumatic drill went away about 6.0 o'clock in the morning but, as far as I was concerned, the night was gone.

The third night I went to a party and looked on the wine when it was red. There were some characters there in white jackets and a great deal of gold braid wheeling trolleys about the place laden with tasty morsels and titbits most tender. But best of all there was the scampi. I think if ever I were to be expecting a baby I would wake up in the night craving for scampi, so maybe it is a good job there is no chance of my ever expecting a baby. I am very partial to scampi.

One of the characters in charge of a trolley eventually recognised this and he said to me: 'If you eat too much of that it'll spoil your dinner.'

So I said to him, 'This is my dinner, brother.'

I think my kind face and gentlemanly manner must have appealed to him. Thereafter he never moved far from my whereabouts with his trolley and he saw to it that I was well plied with scampi.

After this convivial evening my condition was such that all the pneumatic drills in the world wouldn't have kept me awake. But they weren't necessary. Because, as I rolled into bed, the whole menagerie collapsed beneath me. It was a frightening experience.

Had the mattress been flat on the floor I could have coped. But it wasn't. It was lurching crazily at an angle of forty-five degrees so that remedial action was imperative. Normally I'm not a bad hand at making up a bed. But in the early hours of the morning when my faculties are just ever so slightly impaired maybe I don't do it so good.

All through what was left of the night my feet stuck out through the bottom of the bed and therewith went my last hope of fighting off the cold which had been remorselessly creeping up on me. During the fourth night, with the mattress once again *in situ*, I sneezed so violently that sleep was still impossible.

My cup of sorrow was filled to the brim on my last night when I went to the opera. As you know I am very partial to the old doh-ray-me, and no matter what opera is on I will go to see it and enjoy it. So I didn't bother to find out what opera was on.

Well, in fact, I think it is a gross slander on such characters as Verdi, Puccini and Rossini, and in fact a great hoax on one and all to call this stuff opera. It was a thing called Peter Grimes and was nothing but a diabolical noise, only worse than the pneumatic drill which had previously been sent to torment me,

What really upset me, however, was that there were some very good singers in it, and I was surprised to see them allowing themselves to be associated with such cacophony. At the end of the first act I handed in my cloakroom ticket, recovered my coat, put it on, muttered a fearful oath and walked out.

I'm told that this was written, if such is the word, by a Mr Benjamin Britten.* I am also told that Mr Britten is still alive and not an old man, so that there would seem to be a considerable danger of his writing other such dreadful stuff. Well, if they want to turn people against opera that's the way to do it, and give me the Beatles any day.

According to the story on the programme this character Peter Grimes was going to be drowned in the last act, but I couldn't wait that long. In fact I think it was a great shame that he wasn't drowned at the beginning of the first act, and then the whole thing needn't have happened.

Not a very propitious week. Ah, well. Never mind. You can't win 'em all. Perhaps we'll do better at Smithfield.

---

* Many people, including the writer, couldn't stand Benjamin Britten's opera *Peter Grimes*. Whilst many people felt the same about the so-called singing by the pop group known as the Beatles, it was an indictment to mention them both in the same context.

Welsh Farm News, 16 November 1963

It was the sort of thing which could have caused bother but, not for the first time, it passed off all right in the end and everything's under control and everybody is quite happy. I think so anyway.

It's about the Council and the lavatory bucket.

The Clerk said afterwards that he guessed there'd be trouble when he heard the tone of the discussion before the meeting started. Some character by the name of Fanny Hill, it was stated, had just come out with what was expected to be the greatest best-seller since Lady Chatterley wrote her famous book about penguins.

Naturally enough this caused a great deal of interest because there are still some great readers on the Council, in spite of the worst influence of the idiot's lantern. In fact this subject was still in its last throes of muttered discussion by the sub-committee in the corner by the fire when the matters arising had been disposed of, and the Clerk stated that there was nothing under correspondence.

The next item was a report from the fraternal delegate who had attended the triennial conference of Parish Councils in London. Unfortunately, the usual hard core of sporadic attenders had put in an appearance because, with an election due next year, they were getting a bit anxious in view of the unwritten rule concerning fifty per cent attendance.

As usual, they were determined to make their presence felt. First of all the fraternal delegate thanked members for having sent him to this conference and then went on to report on what some titled lady had said. It seems that, because of all the publicity about Christine Keeler and this and that and one thing and another, there was some concern being expressed as to whether there was any danger of prostitution being started in the rural areas.

But apparently the titled lady had ventured the opinion that the danger was only very slight because it was a fact which was well-known to one and all that the rural areas were so well-endowed with enthusiastic amateurs that there was very little chance of professionals being able to make it worthwhile and therefore spoil the good name of the rural areas.

One of the sporadic attenders immediately butted in on what he claimed was a point of order and said that this sounded like a great slander, such as the time when the Chairman had said that the Vice-chairman's mother was a chicken stealer. And, as members would recall, this had resulted in the resignation of the church organist, and culminated in a resounding vote of confidence in the President of the Women's Institute, just when members were in high hopes of getting rid of her.

The Clerk advised, however, that what the titled lady was reported as saying in this case was not *per se* of such a defamatory nature as the allegation of chicken stealing, which was altogether a far more serious accusation. The Chairman therefore ruled the sporadic attender out-of-order and invited the fraternal delegate to continue with his report. But not before there was a further interruption from the sub-committee in the corner by the fire who demanded the publication of a list of amorous wives.

The fraternal delegate then explained that when the titled lady had made this reference at the conference it was only in the form of a joke, and the sporadic attenders obviously felt that they had gained a moral victory. He then continued with his report and his next mention was of some scheme being introduced which would enable Parish Councils to spend up to the product of a fifth of a penny rate on various matters where they couldn't get the proper authorities to move.

Thereupon one of the members of the sub-committee in the corner by the fire suggested that they purchase for each member a copy of the book by Fanny Hill.

The fraternal delegate, however, pressed on regardless to his next item which was about the bucket. And here, to their great credit, even the sub-committee in the corner by the fire fell silent. The fraternal delegate then went on to report that at the conference there had been a big to-do about school sanitation and three cases were quoted where schools were without water and had bucket lavatories.

Rather surprisingly, he said, a medical officer of health had spoken in favour of this arrangement but had been shouted down. The sporadic attenders thereupon demanded to know what was the latest position about their own closet and, on forcing a vote, succeeded in getting the Council to resolve itself *en bloc* into an *ad hoc* tŷ-bach sub-committee to carry out an *in situ* inspection of same. The Clerk explained that the present arrangement was of long-standing. The contents of each bucket were recognised as one of his 'perks', being a most excellent additive for the rhubarb bed.

He had found over the years, however, that it was unwise to overdo it and every third year he used it under the plum tree.

It was wonderful stuff, he said. Grew rhubarb as thick as your arm and plums as big as your two fists. Worth far more than this here new-fangled stuff that was coming in paper sacks.

One of the sporadic attenders, however, pointed out that there was no bolt on the door which might give rise to a certain amount of worry. But the Clerk said there was no need to worry at all. There was no great demand for it these days. Newcomers to the country areas didn't know the worth of it. He couldn't remember when they had lost the last bucketful.

As I said, there could have been a lot of bother. But fortunately the sub-committee in the corner by the fire pointed out that if they didn't pack up and go home they wouldn't see Miss World being judged on television.

Their motion that the meeting be terminated was supported by the usual contingent, who were thinking in terms of closing time, and it was therefore carried by an overwhelming majority *nem con*.

So, like I said, everything passed off all right. But only just. 'Twas a near thing.

---

24 May 1956

Double Dutch

The bank manager had just telephoned the farmer to talk to him like a Dutch uncle.

"But tell me," says the farmer, "what was the position this time last year?"

"This time last year," said the bank manager, "you were in credit."

"Quite so," said the farmer, "and I never phoned you."

Welsh Farm News, 1 February 1964

I don't wish nobody no harm like. Never did. But thinking I am. And no wonder. It's enough to make you think.

News cometh of proposed increases for the civil servants which will mean an increase in their salaries of ten per cent over the next three years. The civil servants seem to be not too pleased about this, but have apparently accepted it on the assurance that the position will be reviewed in 1966.

The reason for their dissatisfaction is the fact that other people have been awarded greater increases and the civil servants seem to have an idea that they are of some use to the rest of the community. Well, maybe if they're thick-skinned enough to live with the stigma of being civil servants, they're entitled to think some kind thoughts about themselves just in case nobody else does.

The trouble at Margam where the steel dispute continues seems to be that one very commendable set of hard-working gentlemen are dissatisfied because some other very commendable and hard-working gentlemen in the same establishment are earning more.

The first bunch of commendable gentlemen do not seem to be concerned so much with how they are faring themselves. Their abiding belly-ache is how the other chap is doing.

There might be no harm in passing if I pointed out the tremendous importance of this column to the continued existence of Farm News. Without it the paper would simply fold up and perish and, because of this, it is beyond price. Mind you, the chances are the Editor doesn't agree with this point-of-view. And, to add insult to injury, the very patient types who put the words into print and all that jazz are no doubt quite sure that without their services our efforts would all come to nought.

In fairness, I should also say that they have never asked me how much I am paid, and I haven't the faintest idea what they earn. But I hope it's enough. If not, I hope they will let me know and I shall be very pleased to write a powerful piece on their behalf. Because I am greatly anxious that they should be keen to go on setting the erudite wisdom which so freely courses from this pen.

So, you see, we all have our uses. And it's rather beginning to look as if we get, not what we are worth, but what we can persuade those who pay us into giving us.

Would it not, then, be so much better, if the NAAS are really going to try to teach us anything at all, if they taught us on something where they are obviously qualified. In fact, instead of trying to persuade us how to cut our own throats with amalgamation and God-knows what-else and put most of our number on the scrap heap or unemployment market, why do they not show us just how an overstaffed and largely useless section of the community (referring to the whole Civil Service, of course) can contrive thus to increase their remuneration and conditions of employment (and holidays) out of all proportion to their work.

If the NAAS could show us some way of getting what we want we'd be greatly obliged I'm sure. Indeed I have some very good friends in the NAAS. Quite excellent types. Kind fathers and good husbands. And if they could just pass on the wrinkle as to how it is done we'd be better friends still. In fact we'd even be in a better position to find our share of the taxes from which the Civil Service increase of £40 millions over the next three years will have to be found.

Welsh Farm News, 13 January 1964

'Ben Brock and the Civil Service.'

Ben Brock is as entitled to his opinion that the Civil Service is an 'over-staffed and largely useless section of the community' as I am to mine that the quasi-Old Testament-Rustic style which he affects is boring and laborious.

But I must ask him to substantiate his suggestion that the pay increase has been accompanied by 'improved conditions of employment and holidays.' All I know is that the claim for the cut in one hour in the working week was rejected.

W. Thomas, Glan Padarn,
Caradog Road, Aberystwyth.'

Welsh Farm News, 15 February 1964

Not for the first time in my life I have been taken to task. This time by Mr W. Thomas, who writes from Aberystwyth, one of the traditional backwater haunts of the ungainfully employed, expressing quite permissible and understandable disapprobation of my passing comments on the Civil Service.

He also expresses certain opinions on the style which, as he puts it, I sometimes affect. Let me hasten to say that all that concerns me is that he has an opinion. What that opinion happens to be is not my most pressing worry just at the moment. It is, however, considerably gratifying that he is in a position to express an opinion, because it means that he has at least read my poor miserable offerings.

I don't want to sound ungracious about this but, as far as opinion on any particular style is concerned, I gave up worrying long ago about what any individual thought or was likely to think. For one thing, it is the function of this column to entertain sometimes, as well as to put the world to rights much of the time, whilst offering some pungent comment on matters topical in between times.

Some folks like one style and some dislike another. Some like a little bit of doggerel and parody, whilst some can't abide it. It takes all sorts to make a world, and I can only say that the style to which Mr Thomas objects is just about the most popular of all, especially amongst people of discernment whose opinions I respect.

To put it as briefly as I can, let me say that I would never hope to be able to please all of the people all the time or even some of the time. I doubt even whether I could ever hope to be able to please some of the people all the time. But if I can please some of the people some of the time I shall be content.

Having disposed of that point we come to the second point, which is a question of content matter. Now Mr Thomas may find this hard to believe, but there really are many people who are quite delighted to see a scribe draw attention to the way in which the Civil Service becomes an increasing burden on the rest of the community.

The folks who are thus delighted are producers who have to provide the wherewithal to keep the increasing hordes of civil servants in the manner to which they have become accustomed. I make no apology for reminding you once again that the wealth of any nation is in what it can produce.

There are those of our number whose function it is to give a service. But these services have to be paid for. And it should be open to the producers who provide the cash to ask how much it is costing, and what sort of service are they getting for their money.

In writing this column I produce nothing which is of any value whatsoever to the rest of the community. But I do provide a service by providing them with something to idle away the leisure hours, either on a Sunday afternoon if they happen to be farmers, or in between tea-breaks if they happen to be civil servants.

They decide for themselves whether they wish to avail themselves of this service, and whether they think it is worth paying for. My only way of interpreting their wishes in the matter is by whether or not the paper remains solvent and continues to pay me.

Well, I'm still here, ain't I?

With the civil servants, however, it is an entirely different matter. We no longer have any choice, because the whole thing has gone completely out of control. The civil servants run the country as surely as the local government officials run the county, district, urban and borough councils.

It is an unfortunate sign of the times that

Parkinson's Law is regarded as a joke. If you think that it's any sort of a joke you should go and read it again.

Take, for example a few facts and figures to which attention is drawn. The officials at the Admiralty increased from 2,000 in 1914 to 3,569 in 1928. During that same period the Navy diminished by a third in men and two thirds in ships. By 1935 the Admiralty staff had increased to 8,118, and by 1954 there were 33,788 of them.

In 1935 the staff at the Colonial Office numbered 372. By 1954 they had increased to 1,661, but Parkinson doesn't by any means suggest that the Empire also grew in that time.

His Law, in case you didn't know, is that 'Work expands so as to fill the time available for its completion.'

Some day somebody might find out what happened to the permanent civil servants concerned with food rationing when food rationing ceased. The best advice they can offer farmers, however, is to work out means whereby they can reduce their staff.

Maybe you don't think the Admiralty or the Colonial Office concern us very much except insofar as the rate of taxation is concerned. And it's no doubt asking a bit much to try to trace those who were once concerned with food rationing and are now sorting out forms somewhere else. Unfortunately, Parkinson doesn't seem to have turned his penetrating attention to the Min. of Ag. and Fish., but there's no reason why we shouldn't give them a thought.

We all know as milk producers that one thing which has bedevilled our livelihood since the war has been the determination of the Ministry to fix the price of milk, which has meant the lunatic up and down a halfpenny a pint at the various seasons of the year.

I have it on the best of authority that this is for no other reason than that there happens to be a handful of civil servants sculling about in some honeycombed retreat whose job during the war was to fix the price of milk and who have so far succeeded in convincing those above them that this is still necessary.

For the sake of such parasites the interest of an entire great and vital industry must be jeopardised.

However, tempus is fidgeting, and there remains one point in Mr Thomas's letter which I have not answered. I am no civil servant, so I must not prevaricate and fail to give a positive answer.

He asks me to substantiate my suggestion that the civil service pay increase has been accompanied by improved conditions of employment and holidays. He can take anything I wrote out of its context to his heart's content, but if he will go back to what I originally wrote he will see that I said nothing of the sort.

I didn't make any mention that they had their last increase in salary only nine moths ago, but I did draw attention to the fact that the civil servants had improved their salaries, conditions of employment and holidays to a state where the remuneration and lack of holidays of the vast majority of those who employ them, that is to say the producers, constitutes a national scandal.

Most of the civil servants I know get six weeks' holiday, whilst they work, if that is the word for it, a five-day forty-four hour week. The tea-making grades, I believe, only get about three weeks holiday. And if anyone feels that these conditions need improving in face of what farmers get, then, by God, he should go and get his sense of values put right.

Just how far out is their sense of values, and just how sure of themselves some of them have become was brought home to me the other day when I heard a District Adviser in the NAAS*, not for the first time, assert that farmers were now an encumbrance to the national economy.

He deplored the fact that he knew one particular farmer, and he knew it from this farmer's costings, who was earning as much as the NAAS man, who seemed to think that this was a scandalous state of affairs, and he was only partially mollified when it was pointed out to him that the farmer had to work twice as many hours to do it.

He further propounded the view that it would be better for the country if we were to import all our food. I have no objection whatsoever to his cutting his own throat to the extent of working himself out of a job. The poor fool no doubt thinks he would be absorbed into some other warm and well-ventilated building in the mistaken belief that the economy can go on carrying this sort of thing indefinitely.

A fat lot his salary would be worth to him if the only producers in the country were some of the other industries we know of, and also the Beatles.

Yeah! Yeah! Yeah!

---

* NAAS: National Agricultural Advisory Service, pronounced Nass, so it was by no means unusual when speaking or writing of them to say 'Forget not the N'.

Welsh Farm News, 28 March 1964

For some time now I have been far from happy about the attitude of salesmen towards agriculture.

Representatives of the trade, I am afraid, are just not with it. There are enough of them, far more than enough, and I think we must be a most remarkable and efficient industry to carry so many 'hidden' passengers upon our weary backs.

But do they woo us enough? Not on your sweet Nelly, they don't. You look at the way they woo the housewife, figuratively speaking that is, and compare it with the lack of interest displayed towards the farmer.

But I have ideas about this. I've been thinking. Not furiously, nor yet profoundly. But thinking, all the same.

First of all, there's the milking. A regular chore, like wash-day for the housewife on Monday. Well, we all know about that one because we've seen on the old goggle-box how it's done. So what I want now is for somebody to come knocking at our door and say: 'Have you a milking machine?'

And, of course, I will say yes I have a milking machine, and as a matter of fact it is an Omega Sanitary type which is very popular with one and all.

So then this character will say: 'Would you like us to do your twice-a-day milking for you for three weeks?'

And unless you're a complete dairy nut case, you will say for him to come inside most immediate.

Then you discover the only point in his asking you whether you have a milking machine is for him to know whether he can demonstrate or not.

Otherwise he will be like the bloke flogging vacuum cleaners, who tips a bag of soot on the carpet and then asks where the plug is, only to be told that they become fed up with the constant power cuts as soon as the weather turns cold, so they go in for all gas. I don't suppose the farm demonstrator will like to sit down and milk by hand twice a day for three weeks to do his demonstrating.

And what he has come to demonstrate is the new improved wonder Dairy Snow with extra blue in it, as well as the new, miracle cleaner XYZ 123. The combination of this new miracle cleanser and the extra blue make Dairy Snow the most effective powder on the market, unsurpassed for value by all other imitations.

In fact, Dairy Snow is so complete that it not only eats into the corners of every claw and cluster, but there is positively no need to add ammonia to it, unless you want to alter the smell, which may be necessary if you happen to put the bucket down too close behind the wrong cow at the wrong time in the wrong place.

But this is not all. So confident are the makers of new Dairy Snow that they recently hold an election to find out what exactly farmers think of their wonderful product. And the results of the poll just announced show that, out of the 500 who vote, no fewer than 491 think that Dairy Snow is definitely the greatest.

Although it has been discovered that such elections can be rigged by the canvassers making a two way split with any floating voters, it is considered likely that the figures are almost certainly genuine, because most farmers I know will vote as being greatly in favour of anybody willing to do their twice-a-day milking for them for three weeks.

Of the nine who vote against, one is still trying to get enough money together to pay for last year's National Health stamps,* one is waiting until Huw T. Edwards** will give the scheme his blessing by giving away some more Welsh dolls, two think such a scheme will contribute still further to the problem of the depopulation of rural Wales, two think they could get it cheaper through the group, two are not for us and are therefore assumed to be against us, whilst the ninth admits that he just wants to be bloody awkward.

You see what I mean. The potential is fantastic. There must be a complete re-appraisal of the position and a new approach demanded. We must ask for much more than merely being allowed to listen to one gramophone record before buying some more insurance.

Nothing less than the Philarmonia lined up in the field for a fortnight will do from now on.***

---

* Employers were supposed to stamp the National Health Insurance cards of their employees each week.
** Huw T Edwards, Chairman of the recently formed Wales Tourist Board, or some such organisation, as far as I remember, and giving away little Welsh dolls was something of a promotional gimmick.
*** To understand reference to Philharmonia see p. 87 of *A Rural Miscellany*, (Gwasg Carreg Gwalch, 2006).

Welsh Farm News, 4 April 1964

It seems that from now on the Small Farm Scheme will not be taking up quite as much of the time of the enthusiastic advisory gentlemen as has been the case for the last half-dozen years or so. Apparently the next emphasis is to be on business management and all that jazz. So, if you ask me, we shall need to be very much on our guard. And I start thinking on these lines because the other day I meet up with a wild-eyed character with no end of problems.

In fact he is so full of problems that the NAAS are liable to offer him advice with considerable energy. But I do not think he will be likely to take much advice from anybody, because I hear him holding forth recently and he states that if it is not for his being so foolish as to go along with some NAAS advice that he will now be about £3,000 better off.

Now I think this is a very wild statement to make, but I am not in a position to challenge him as he keeps many pages of figures ready to hand and can always prove to you how badly he is doing. So I merely say is that so, which does not exactly contradict him, but does indeed seem to encourage him more than somewhat.

Because he gets me in a corner and states as follows: 'I am thinking about you recently,' he says, 'and I work out something which I think will be of interest to your readers if you will make some mention of it some time in your comic strip.'

Then he proceeds to argue as follows, but not before he has spoken with great disrespect of the NAAS in general and their ideas of business management in particular. He states that the one aim of the NAAS is to show how a farmer can manage with less labour. In fact, once they can get a farmer with a viable set-up all on his own, the NAAS are very happy because there is then no hope left for the farmer whatsoever and the next step is to tell him he must be amalgamated.

And it is a fact which is well-known to one and all that small farmers are much more efficient, and produce much more per acre per cent per man perhaps than the big farmers, so that the politicians, who are generally very wicked types to be sure, are anxious to encourage a great deal of amalgamation to have less production to embarrass them, and then they can import as much as they like.

So this character then goes on to state that the next move with the NAAS is to show how a farm can be run as a business with just the farmer and one man, because this does away with the argument of drudgery and enables everybody to take time off to eat cream buns, or whatever happens to be their wish in these matters, such as going to the seaside and taking off their shoes and socks and rolling up their trousers to go paddling with the infants.

Now, the idea seems to be that if a farmer employs one man he will have to keep at least 60 or 70 cows to keep himself and his man in the manner to which they would like to become accustomed. And provided they pull their finger out, and pay due attention to the old time-and-motion, they can maybe run things pretty good between them.

This explains about business management and work study, and you will naturally expect the farmer and his man to be considerably pleased about this arrangement. But you must remember that it is laid down in the book, and must at all times be complied with, that the workman must have 15 days holiday during the year.

I am a great supporter of this system myself as it affords a great opportunity for the workman to dig the garden, or go off to see some uncles and cousins and other such characters, and generally come back to work feeling much refreshed.

Now, any self-respecting working farmer likes to feel that he is just as much entitled to such a holiday as this himself, which is another 15 days, amounting to 30 days in all between the farmer and his workman. On top of that, there are five bank holidays during the year, and the workman will wish to avail himself of this statutory privilege.

The farmer, fair play, will think along similar lines, which will mean another five days, making ten days in all. So you will see that for 48 weeks of the year there will be nobody on holiday, and even farmworkers are entitled to expect at least one day off a week. Naturally, the farmer will cotton on to this idea, which means another 48 days each, or 96 days in all. So if you reckon up the 30 days for holidays proper, the ten days for bank holidays and the 96 days for days off you will have a total of 136 days.

In language which you and I are likely to understand this means that there are 136 days of the year on which there will be only one man on the farm to do the work of two men. Or, if you want it another way, there will be 136 days of the year on which it will be impossible to do anything but the bare essentials, and any seasonal operations will have to be given a miss.

This explains about business management. And I understand about this argument because a NAAS character explains it to me the other day, and he also goes on to state something else which I find to be most disturbing.

He states that he goes through many sets of costings on dairy farms in his time on many differing systems including self-feed silage and large lumps of efficiency. But he makes a remarkable discovery of a factor which is common to all of them.

And then he states that he discovers that whichever system is being operated the people who are making

101

the most money are the people who have the best cows. And if you consider that it is necessary to set up the NAAS in order to discover this, I hope and trust you will consider you get great value for your money when you realise that I keep on telling you this for years for only 4d. a week.

But I am worried about this because, now that the NAAS have made this great discovery, it is possible that they will consider it their duty to teach us how to breed better cows. I hate to think what this character who speaks about their business management ideas will have to say about it. But I do not think I will be able to write about it for you because he sometimes uses strong language. He will be very upset.

Welsh Farm News, 4 July 1964

The last time I pen a few lines for you in this column I am in great haste and full of great excitement so that I do not get round to telling you that I am going for a holiday.

And I know from long experience that you always wish me to write of such matters as when I go on holiday. It is also well-known to one and all that, as far as I am concerned, the only place to go for a holiday to get great quantities of peace and quiet is out on an island, where time matters not and where there is nothing to do in between sleeping and eating, except maybe get a bit more sleep.

Maybe some of you will remember that the last time I go for a holiday to one of these remote islands I am accompanied by a character with a slipped disc who has to put drops in his eyes and he also has many cameras. You will also remember how we cure his slipped disc and his bad eyes because he has to wind on the big winch to get the boat out of the sea during a great storm when the salt water is splashing all over his face. Since that time he never looks back and is always in rude good health and forgets all about his slipped disc and his eyedrops.

Well, I meet up with this character one day and he says he now gets over the effects of the last holiday when we have to wind the boat up out of the water in a great storm, and do I not think it is high time for us to take another holiday for him to take lots of pictures of all the beautiful creatures round and about.

Now I never need any encouragement to clear off to an island and am greatly excited at the prospect because it is two years since I have a holiday.

Next thing that happens is that it comes on a Sunday and we meet up with a boatman who takes us over the rolling waves in search of peace and quiet. It is a very nice island and as near uninhabited as makes no difference.

There is one other character there, however, who says he goes to this island as he is in need of building up and the doctor advises him on this matter. And what the doctor tells him is that he must have plenty of steak and swimming and pretty girls. I do not pass any comment about this, but I certainly think that this is such a doctor as I will be very pleased to consult sometime myself.

Even so, I think this character is a little bit mixed up in some of the things he tells us, because he certainly lands up in one hell of an unlikely place as far as finding any pretty girls could be concerned.

Anyway the character with the cameras and I go off in search of pictures, and I am carrying the heavy stuff. Then we come to a sheltered spot near the cliff top and eat some oranges and go fast asleep in the sun.

It is very restful and, I am glad to say, when we wake up there is no time to take any pictures that day because we must cook a meal as you cannot live on oranges nor can you take pictures of all the beautiful creatures on an empty stomach. In this manner our strength returns unto us and we decide we will now challenge the character who has been on the steak to see if the steak is doing him any good.

There is a big iron buoy which has been washed up on the island, and this buoy, with a piece of chain attached to it, weighs about two tons and steakstuffer shows off his strength by lifting this above his head, so we say this is not sufficient. We say the winner will be the one who can throw this buoy the furthest, and we do this by holding the chain in both hands and swinging the buoy round three times and then hurling it with great force.

The character with the cameras goes first and swings round in a very rapid manner, with this great iron buoy at arm's length on the end of the chain, until he feels giddy and the buoy lands about six feet away. And this is a good throw indeed, because the character with the cameras does not remember to let go of the buoy when he throws it.

Then it is my turn and I hurl the buoy about fifteen feet, because by this time my strength is returning to me in great quantities. Last of all comes the character on the steak build-up, and to our great surprise when he tries to throw this iron buoy he can do no better than drop it on his foot. So I tell him to eat some more steak and not think too much about the pretty girls for the time being.

Next day it comes on a fervent heat and I strip off and hurl myself into the clear blue water shouting, oh my gawd this is very cold, but I have to keep swimming as the water round the island is about two thousand feet deep. And I cannot understand why there is so much fuss about the topless bathing costumes because mine does not have a bottom either. It is an enchanting sight, but of course, there is no one there who is likely to pay much attention.

Certainly there are no pretty girls, which is why I say I cannot understand why this character thinks his doctor's advice will do him any good on an island such as this. And when I get to thinking about this problem I remember that the Editor says to me some time ago that I do not write any of my celebrated nonsense just lately and what about it.

So I say to him that in fact I have been thinking about writing a few lines on the scandal which some Professor speaks about concerning wives being swapped between the dayshift and the nightshift workers in a most promiscuous manner. But the Editor does not seem to think that this is a brilliant idea to write of such a matter.

So I say I also consider writing on the subject of the

new laws concerning castration and rubber rings and such matters, and he says do I mean writing about these two subjects in the same column, and I say maybe I could do that as well. And he says he will not put anything past me, and I say I know that but will he print it? And he says he will not express an opinion on this matter until he sees what I wish to write.

So I say I will first of all take a holiday on this island and then when I come back I shall be able to give some thought to such important matters and maybe write a little bit of nonsense.

Welsh Farm News, 14 November 1964

Well, there it is. Not without the odd moments of panic, bonfire night has come and gone once again, and the late Mr. Fawkes can be forgotten for another twelve months.

This year we had a considerable conflagration. Amongst other things the opportunity was taken to burn a mountain of trash from the hedges which have been taking quite a bit of pruning of recent weeks. The weather having held fair for so long, a most burnable material was available in quantity, and young badgers tend to make the best of such opportunities. It was a mighty blaze, aided and abetted by two dozen old tyres.

As zero hour approached, and last minute arrangements were being made as to who was going where to set off their fireworks, I realised why whist drive organisers and other such hardy and enthusiastic characters always display with their advertisements in the local papers, the footnote: 'Other secretaries please note. Please do not clash.'

Fortunately, there is only one November 5th. Once a year is enough to run the risk of dying of heart failure.

As the first volley of sparks cannonaded into the night sky and swept in a menacing flow above the hayshed, I suddenly remembered that I had forgotten to remember to fill the fire extinguisher. The wind had been behaving quite sensibly earlier in the day, although blowing, with a considerable degree of what may reasonably be described as freshness, in a direction away from any likelihood of danger. At the last minute it shifted direction somewhat.

However, to cut a long story short, the fire extinguisher is now primed ready for action. Hence the saying, 'It's an ill wind that blows nobody any good.' Because this extinguisher has been empty since our last spot of bother, which is maybe four or five years ago. And I expect you know how it is with outfits such as this one which is greatly inefficient, as I never weary of telling you.

Now that I've been forced, in quick time at that, to get round to the task of filling the fire extinguisher, I've been toying with the idea of putting up a notice alongside it to say that it is considerably against the law to use it as a hanger for wire, baling twine, sacks, oilskins or anything else for which there seems to be no other place, and the removal of which can cause considerable delay in the event of an emergency.

I shall not put up such a notice, however, because I'm old enough to realise that nobody would take a blind bit of notice. I know. Because I've tried it.

Take the case of the first-aid box, which is now necessary because of laws to this effect, and it is indeed a great crime to be without one. It is also a great crime to have a first-aid box if it is not full of all the specified medicaments.

So the minute you use some of it, you are breaking the law until you fill the box up again, and there is always an even money chance that this is liable to take quite a bit of time as you will realise from the case of the fire extinguisher. Therefore when I finally get round to buying the box, I do the obvious thing and put up a notice alongside it saying that on no account should the box be opened or any of its contents used. It is there purely to avoid breaking the law.

I think the notice must have been thrown away, or something, because I acquire a bit of a burn on my thumb whilst the bonfire antics and fireworks are at their most frantic pitch, which is after the fire extinguisher has been filled, and I look for a bit of sticky plaster in the first-aid box and there is none there.

What happened, I think, was that the ball-joint on

the tractor governor was worn, and it kept dropping off, and the sticky plaster had to be used to bind it up a bit. Either that, or the spout of the corn-drill. My memory isn't as good as all that these days. Neither is anybody else's as far as I can make out.

But it is obvious that the box will have to be filled up again. Just when I was thinking that, having filled the fire extinguisher, I would be able to sit back and take life easy for a while.

There's always something.

---

30 August 1956

The old trick

The baby rabbit had been tormenting its mother all day. You know how they do. In the end the old girl couldn't stand it any longer.

"Well, all right," she said. "If you must know you were pulled out of a conjurer's hat. Now stop asking questions!"

Welsh Farm News, 20 February 1965

A safe income from gilts – That's what it said

This is a column about not much, which is the sort of column I have to write every now and again when there is not much about which to write, and there is certainly not much about which to write at the moment. Wherefore and therefore, this is a column about not much.

I suppose there's the Price Review, but that's been done to death already, and we've even been told what to expect on the various commodities. I wouldn't pretend to know about that. What I reckon is that we might do better than we expect by getting a long overdue increase in the standard quantities.

Apart from anything else it would be above the heads of most of the people who read the daily papers as well as most of those who write for them, so that it would save us from the nonsense of banner headlines saying so many millions more for the farmers.

Well, I cannot pursue this subject any further, and I am very hard pressed for a subject on which to write for you. However, it is well-known to one and all that everybody takes more papers and magazines than ever they will have time to read, and they are all greatly surprised at themselves that they go on taking so many papers.

And now that you come to mention it, I must admit I am in this category myself, although it may come as a surprise to some subjects that I can read at all, but it is certainly an achievement which comes in handy when I wish to write a column for you, especially when it is a column about not much.

The important thing about writing a column like this, however, is to have a subject about which to write, and then have a peg on which to hang it as they say.

Now I don't know whether you're anything like I am, but I am very partial to reading the papers when they are on the floor. It is the custom in some establishments to put old newspapers down on the floor when the floor has been washed, or if there is a spot of decorating going on, or other such matters, and I find it is quite remarkable what interesting items there are in the papers at such times.

It is by no means unusual for me to see a headline under the dinner-table and get down on my hands and knees to read same, only to finish with a kick up the crumpet from Mrs Brock, who says supper is ready, but I am bound to state it is never a very hard kick. It is the principle of the thing which counts.

On the other hand it is also likely at such times that you come across one of the papers which you hardly ever open, and then you find that it is nothing but a load of old rubbish, and you wonder more than ever why you go on taking it.

It is when I am wondering what I can write about for you which will be of some interest that I see a headline which says 'A MORE SAFE INCOME FROM GILTS'. Needless to say, so why say it, I drop down on my hands and knees the same as if I am shot, because this is a matter which is bound to be of very great interest to one and all including yours truly.

In fact it is of particular interest to yours truly, because I now read so much of what I read about the dangers of specialisation that I finally convince myself that what I am saying must be correct, and so recently I haul off and buy myself a couple of gilts, and very nice gilts they are at that.

Well, naturally, I am greatly excited to see such a headline to prove that I am on to a good thing, and nothing pleases me more than to see an article stating that there is a safe income in gilts. If there is one thing I will appreciate more than any other just at this moment it is a safe income from anything, and I consider myself very wise and far-sighted to have ensured a safe income by buying these gilts.

Mind you, I do not expect too much because many of these articles are by professors and such characters, not to mention NAAS advisers, and nobody ever reads them to any great extent. But I get down on my knees and prop my chin up with my hands, and then I see that this article is not even by a NAAS adviser, but is only by a Special Correspondent.

However, no matter who is writing about the subject, I think I will be greatly interested to learn some more about a safe income from gilts, and so I commence to read. But it turns out they are different gilts from what I have, because the gilts* I have either eat up food out of a bag if you keep them in, or go causing more trouble than somewhat if you turn them out. We are not organised.

And the gilts about which the Special Correspondent is writing are gilt-edged securities such as Government stocks and shares and all that jazz, with many references to 21/2 per cent, the Treasury and the Labour Government, which is no more interesting than the articles by the professors and the NAAS advisers and such characters.

Certainly I do not think this will be a suitable subject for me to write a column which you will wish to read. And that is why the column this week is about not much.

So now you know.

---

* Gilts: young female pigs, usually those which have not yet had a litter. As opposed to the other gilts, which are 'gilt-edged securities such as Government stocks and shares and all that jazz'.

Welsh Farm News, 26 June 1965

TV, Beatles and other Island Thoughts

Where was I? Now let me see. Ah, yes, that's right. I was talking about the times of the milk lorry calling and all that jazz before concluding by telling you that I was away to the islands.

If I remember rightly I said that there would be no telephone, no postman. Only large lumps of solitude where time matters not. And that's the way it is. Better still, there is no goggle-box nor even a transistor radio.

This year, at the eleventh hour, Mrs. Brock relented and agreed to the entreaties of one small badger to be allowed to accompany his lunatic, mad-brained father on one of these idiotic sorties across rough waters to live on a 'barren old rock'. Nonsense, my dear. It's a lovely place.

I was saying about the goggle-box though. How they brain-wash you without your realising it. When I was laying in stores for this sojourn in solitude I bought, just to try, one of the marvellous curries about which they're always telling you. And now we've tried it. Mark you, I'm not blaming the curry. But it wasn't a success.

After the rice was well and truly boiling in a pint and a half of salted water, I read where you have to finish up by putting it through a colander or sieve. Well, we didn't happen to have a colander or sieve, so we did the next best thing we could. We poured it through the tea-cloth.

I'm willing to admit for that matter that the tea-cloth had seen better days, but beggars can't be choosers and it was the only one we had. Simmering the curry part of the concoction for twenty minutes, whilst keeping covered and giving a gentle stir also presents its problems. From now on I reckon it will be better to cut out the fancy stuff.

However, I was saying about time mattering not and no postman and so on. Yesterday a boatman gave us a shout and said would we like the paper? This has been an event to enable us to catch up with things.

I see the team for the Second Test with the New Zealanders has been announced, and Barrington has been dropped. Ah well, that's the way it goes. I'm also somewhat taken with the business of the Beatles getting the MBE. So what? Why all the fuss?

Like I've always said, I'm very partial to the old doh-ray-me, and I think the Beatles make one hell of a noise, which is why such badgers as yours truly have to try to find places like this to get away from it and have a chance to retain their sanity.

But don't blame the Beatles. Blame the morons for whom they provide this cacophony. I'm told that of their kind they're very good. By taking money off the masses they've amassed great wealth. Gentlemen in the City do the same thing by means of legalised spivvery and give some of it away to avoid tax and get honours conferred on them accordingly.

This is regarded as strictly legitimate, so can anyone tell me what's the difference? Furthermore the whole daft business has been reduced to such a farce over recent years that I don't think anybody bothers any more whether such honours go to the right people or not. They do occasionally, but how often?

I was watching some razorbills and guillemots on a cliff ledge yesterday. Whilst I found their antics very fascinating I'm bound to admit that their reactions seemed to be more predictable than those of the human species. But that's life isn't it?

If this ever sees the light of day you'll know I'm back safe and sound. And I hope that it won't make you nearly as sad as it will make me. If you know what I mean.

Welsh Farm News, 3 July 1965

Home Again Safe And Sound

Well, like I said, if the last effort saw the light of day it would signify that I was back again safe and sound and that's the way it is. Back anyway. Maybe the safe and sound would warrant further investigation and analysis, because some folks would reckon I've never been very sound anyway.

And now I'm not so sure about the safe. Fortunately, Mrs. Brock is not much given to violence but, after what I write about the curry, she reckons I ought to be crowned with the saucepan. It's the young badger she was worrying about, and she didn't think much of the idea of straining the boiled rice through a tea-cloth. In fact, she gave me quite a bit of the old theory on germs and that.

So I said there was no need to worry about that side of it, because the rice had been well boiled. But it was the cloth she was thinking about, so then I had to explain that I knew the cloth was perfectly clean because I'd had to wash it out two days previously after using it to straighten things out after a Welsh rarebit had point blank refused to co-operate.

If you ask me, I reckon there's a lot of old guff talked about this sort of thing. Take the milk business, for example. All this old fuss about licenses and measurements and rules and regulations. As if they matter to the consumer. All the housewife bothers about is whether the milk she buys is sweet and wholesome and will keep without too much fuss until she has a chance to use it.

Mark you, I'm not saying that the rules and regulations don't do anybody any good, because look at all the characters who get a living out of enforcing them. The simple answer of sending back any milk not bang up to the standard is far too simple to appeal to a nation whose regard for its producers pales into insignificance beside the way it heaps largesse upon those whom the producers have to carry.

So the same thing must surely apply to straining boiled rice through a tea-cloth. It's the result that counts. And by result, I don't mean the curry. I mean the strong healthy young badger nourished on such dishes. The proof of the curry is in the eating as the saying goes.

Welsh Farm News, 11 December 1965

Time they appointed the Scramble Committee

So it's three cheers for Brambell* whose report is published and now almost everybody is almost happy about almost everything. Or almost-anyway.

Certainly the main point is appreciated which is that the culprits responsible for precipitating large doses of factory farming are the people who have been demanding cheaper food. The fact that animals or birds are kept under intensive conditions does not in itself mean that there is cruelty going on.

Indeed there are no doubt countless cases of creatures being kept under traditional conditions and being neglected to an extent which makes their so-called factory farm counterparts look very well-off and without any cause to complain whatsoever.

However, I do not wish to write for you at any great length on this subject this week because, now that friend Brambell and his committee dispose of the factory farming issue, there is a much bigger problem waiting to be tackled.

And it needs to be tackled immediately, if not sooner, because it involves the most diabolical cruelty anybody could imagine and the time has arrived to do something about it. And it is well-known to one and all that I am a great believer in exposing wickedness and injustice at all times, and therefore that is why I wish to speak of this matter at this time.

This all comes about because I am now in London in order that I can make observations various on the great Smithfield Show, since this is one of the big agricultural occasions of the year, with all the prime bullocks and fat lambs and pork pigs, and you never see such a magnificent parade of tender succulence in all your Nelly.

But I do not wish to speak of this matter, otherwise I will have no time left to speak of all the diabolical wickedness which it is high time someone exposed. And what I am concerned about is the way they treat the people in this place. What is even more frightening is the fact that the people seem to become conditioned to being treated in this way, and will hardly say thank you if you try to treat them any other way.

In fact many of them live in cubicles all stuck one on top of each other, and they call them flats. But they are not flat at all. In fact they are very steep, both in height and in price. When they leave these flats, where they live by night, they go to spend the day in more cubicles with hordes of other people.

What is more, they are so determined to make sure that no opportunity to suffer is lost or left to chance that they fill these cubicles with stinking, filthy smoke so that their eyes run and they cough and then they can get cancer and be whipped away into bigger places with more cubicles and be cut about before being put in a box out of the way out of it all.

Before this can happen, however, they have to travel back and fore and to and fro between the set of cubicles where they live by night and the set of cubicles where they work by day. And this is the most shameful part of the whole business and greatly in need of being exposed.

In fact some of the younger female characters seem to be quite determined to do some exposing on their own account, but this is not quite what I have in mind when I speak of some exposure being necessary and called for. It is all a great scandal. I will go so far as to say that the transport between cubicles is diabolical in its cruelty. Everybody is packed in tighter than sardines, and it is all most alarming especially if you are troubled with not being able to draw your breath very good.

118

And any time you wish to get your hand free to blow your nose, by the time you find your handkerchief you are quite likely to have undone the braces of the character who is packed in next to you. But if it is one of the young female characters who is packed in next to you they will not be wearing braces. However, as likely as not they will be wearing stiletto heels, which I suppose are some kind of self-defence against such characters as will wish to discover whether they are wearing braces or not. I do not ever wish to discover about the braces myself, because I am once trodden on by a stiletto heel.

If there is any worse pain in this world I never wish to experience it. But it is time for all this business to be sorted out, and I await the appointment and terms of reference of the Scramble Committee with very great interest indeed.

---

* Professor Brambell was Chairman of the committee appointed to look into the business of factory farming and the keeping of poultry in cages, or batteries as they are sometimes known.

Welsh Farm News, 19 March 1966

I think it would be just as well, before we go any further, to tell you to keep the paper out of the way of maiden aunts and other such high-minded characters this week.

I rather fear that this column is about to take one of those occasional falls from grace for which it is notorious. I make no apologies about this, but merely give fair warning in advance. I propose to write about lavatories.

Sometimes it is called a closet or toilet or cloakroom. Then again there is the more sophisticated expression such as the loo, or the more homely name appropriate to the Land of Our Fathers, the tŷ bach. Call it what you like, however, a lavatory is still a lavatory.

It even has its own particular brand of humour, which you can see with certain characters on some of the television shows. There is other humour concerning lavatories which is not in itself lavatory humour. Like the little boy who went into the chemist shop.

He waited patiently for his turn, and then, in front of a shopful of people, and in reply to the chemist's, 'What can I get for you, sonny?' asked please could he have a roll of lavatory paper.

Well, maybe the chemist was taken a little aback and he asked the little lad to stand on one side for a minute. Then, when the shop was empty, he explained to him nicely and kindly that he knew what he meant, but the term was really toilet paper and this was how nice people referred to it. Toilet paper.

So the little boy said, yes, he would remember that and thank you very much.

A couple of weeks later he came into the shop again. Once more in front of a shopful of people the chemist asked him what he wanted.

'Please can I have a bar of soap?' said the young customer.

Smiling and rubbing his hands the chemist said, 'Toilet soap?'

'No,' said the lad, 'Mammy wants to wash her face'.

However, I digress. I started thinking about all this because of a little news item that a customer had ordered a mink-covered seat for his concern, and the report was therefore headed, 'Mink for the loo'.

I have no intention of opening up a vast discussion on the hygienic aspects of the matter, nor do I intend that there should be any play on the word 'aspects'. I would go as far as to say that, under certain circumstances, the comfort of the arrangement could be considerable.

Like when you're burning with a raging fever, and a cold seat can come as a nasty old shock to the system. This is the price of progress and they danged old plastic seats. There never were no complaints about the far more comfortable bench-type arrangement down in the garden. Maybe the occasional splinter, but no coldness.

However, the disturbing thing about all this is that the customer for the mink covered seat for his loo, at a cost, mark you, of about £20, is reported to have been a farmer. Yes, a farmer. Could base treachery sink any lower?

Never mind what the public will think and say about the subsidies and the feather-bedding. Let them shout about the mink-padded lavatory seats as well. But, what about the home producer? What are the Wool Board doing about it?

Surely 'Lamb's wool for the loo' must be the slogan. It will be too late when the mink craze has caught on. Now is the time for us to do something about it. And I offer the idea free, gratis and for nothing. I'm like that, as I've told you before.

Come to think of it, you might just as well ask your maiden aunts what they think about the idea. They, too, have their moments.

Welsh Farm News, 2 May 1968

You may remember that I explain for you in this column a week or so ago how it comes about that I sometimes write for you in one fashion and sometimes in another.

So, what with one thing and another, I never know from one week to the next what fashion, or indeed what subject, will crop up next. It all depends on how I'm feeling. And at such times as this when there is nothing immediately pressing about which to write, then I am always apt to write such a column as people will say is a very great load of old rubbish.

I often explain to you that many, many years ago a very wise old editor teaches me the lesson that the weather is a never failing help in time of trouble. Unfortunately, such matters are out of the question this week, because only last week I write for you on this subject saying how beautiful it is to hear the grass growing. And naturally I cannot expect to write on such matters again this week, otherwise the regular customers are apt to put in a very great beef indeed and say to the Editor do you not think he is pushing his luck a bit too far, and is it not time he stirred things up again and pulled down the wrath of somebody or other on his head.

It is unfortunate that I cannot write of these matters, because last week I see my first couple of swallows, and I remember that once upon a time I write a little piece in which I say that even if one swallow doesn't make a summer, then certainly a couple of them make a spring. But since I write about this subject for you some years ago it will never do to write about the same subject again now, otherwise somebody will rake it up and say they wish something better for their money than to have the same old thing hashed up again in some other form.

On the other hand, much as I would like to write a most stirring piece for you about the Rural Dispossession Board,* that is not by any manner or means possible not nohow. We have to be very careful what we say about such matters at this time on account of the laws of *sub judice* and *ipso fatso* and that, which is much the same as being had up for liable and definition of character only more so. And if that happens they can issue a writ against us and have our corpse or something, which sounds like a very nasty old complaint indeed.

The only alternative, therefore, is to go about the place uttering a lot of duck-billed platitudes, and it is a well-known fact that this is why we have to have a nuclear detergent, which is apt to give rise to a case of *ulterior virus*, and that's another nasty old complaint. Still, the proof of the pudding doesn't necessarily make a summer either, and the only thing to do is to take the bull by the horns of the particular dilemma. Which is quite a lot of bull at that, and it means that this week there is nothing to write about whatsoever.

It is at times such as this that I think about those characters who say to me when do you do your writing, and how do you think of something to write about every week? They also say do I write first thing in the morning, or last thing at night, or what? Well, leaving out the what part of it, I am likely to do either, except that I am never very bright in the mornings, and also liable to fall asleep at nights, which doesn't allow much room for manoeuvre in between.

And as to what I do if I don't know what to write about well, of course, I just have to sit there staring out of the window, hoping and praying that something will come, chewing the end of the pen, biting my nails and scratching my bristles, and generally getting worked up into a terrible lather as the deadline approaches.

Then, if nothing turns up, it's like I said, I'm apt to

write such a column as will generally be regarded as a very great load of old rubbish indeed.

On the other hand, the more discerning ones – the intelligent ones for whom I explain to you recently I always reckon I'm writing – say ha, ha, is he not an incorrigible old badger, and the cunning old b----r (badger) has done it again. So now you know.

---

* This is just the writer having a dig at the Rural Development Board.

Welsh Farm News, 7 **September 1968**

We are still just about in what is known in the newspaper business as the silly season and, with your permission, therefore, I would like to revert to the subject of the bees again this week, without writing about the bees if you know what I mean.

Now that we're on the subject, however, I would like to point out in self-defence that, due to one of those little gremlins that manage to get mixed up in the type from time to time, the dear old lady was quoted as saying to the parson, 'Oh, vicar, I didn't know you kept bees!' What she said was, 'I didn't know you kept a bee!'

However, one of the more critical types, who tries to keep this column up to the mark from time to time, says it is obvious I do not know very much about bees otherwise I will never refer to a bee as a he going off to do some work. Well, it is a fact which is well-known to one and all that a he bee has a much nicer life and death than to have to do things like work. But I reckoned that maybe a bee could be referred to as a he occasionally as a figure of speech. And I wasn't really intending to let the question of sex rear its ugly head in this particular case, because there are enough arguments going on all over the place without starting even more trouble inadvertently.

It is necessary for me to say all this, because this character of whom I am now speaking, says since it is obvious I do not know very much about bees will I also be prepared to make it known that I do not know anything about white-fly either. So I say by all means if it will help in a good cause.

It seems that this character is sore troubled by these greatly obnoxious little white-flies, which are borne upon the wind in countless thousands, and come and play merry old pop generally with his tomatoes.

Having sprayed and fumigated and what-not and cleared them out they are as bad as ever again in a couple of days.

In fact, this character says that it probably costs more to get rid of the white-flies than the tomatoes are worth in the first place, because by all account tomatoes are a very poor trade whatever, and look at all the foreign competition anyway.

Now it could be that this business of spraying and fumigating and what-not has more to do with it than would be supposed, because I've heard it said that this is the sort of thing which has been killing off all the little red spiders. And there is an idea going about that, if the little red spiders are not killed off by sprays and that in very great numbers, they will be more than pleased to take care of as many little white-flies as you wish to nominate. In fact, I even hear somebody say the other day that these little white-flies are by no means averse to being killed off by the little red spiders, because if they are left to their own devices they will carry their own supply of little red spiders with them.

Hence it is that best part of three centuries ago Jonathan Swift writes:

'So, naturalists observe, a flea hath smaller fleas that
                                        on him prey,
And these have smaller fleas to bite 'em, and
                                    so proceed ad infinitum.'

And all the time we are thinking he is only really talking about civil servants and parasites various.

Now I hope and trust that it is perfectly obvious from all this that I do not know anything at all worth speaking of about the little white-flies, except that they are playing merry old pop with this character's tomatoes. And he thinks that if only I will write something about it in my blat, as he says, then somebody might come up with a cure.

Perhaps somebody will send him a cartload of little red spiders. But I'm not sure whether that is what he has in mind.

---

6 June 1957

An experiment

An apocryphal story which will appeal to those who do not hold with too much talk of reducing costs of production.

It concerns an experiment which was conducted recently in defiance of the law of diminishing returns. And the experiment was conducted on a horse in order to establish to what extent it was possible to cut down on feeding costs.

Anyway, the horse's feed was weighed carefully and all output figures assiduously recorded. To everyone's entire satisfaction the horse each day had fractionally less to eat but still did as much work as on the previous day.

The scheme continued. The horse had less and less to eat but still did as much work.

When the experiment came to an end it was held to have been conclusive and entirely satisfactory in the facts and figures it had established. "In fact," stated the report, "if the horse had not died…"

Welsh Farm News, 14 December 1968

Ben Takes Time Off To Visit A Football Match

Well there I am in London for the Smithfield Show, and minding my own business in every way whatsoever, when I read in the London blats about a field in North London where there is to be staged a very great outbreak of foot-and-mouth, and I decide I will have a basinful of this spectacle.

In fact, I think this will be a nice change from the opera — although I also see some opera this time, but once again it is the opera about the very big soprano who dies from consumption before they bring in the attested herds scheme, and I write about this for you before. So there is no more to be said on this account because, if I write about the same thing again, people will say it is a load of old rubbish. And whilst they will say it is bad enough to write a load of old rubbish in the first place, they will never stand for having the same load of old rubbish dished up twice.

So this is a load of old rubbish about this field in North London and a very great outbreak of foot-and-mouth, and in fact it is nothing but a football match between two great London rivals called Tottenham Hotspur and Arsenal. And the feeling between some of the supporters of these clubs is so bad that when they start shouting at each other they make some of the FUW* utterances sound as if they are quotations from the Sermon on the Mount.

Now this field is known as White Hart Lane, and it only holds 56,000 people. But twice as many people wish to see this match, so the head bosses decide that it will be an all-ticket affair, and the result is that you will never get in at all unless you can meet up with a gentleman who is known as a tout.

So I set off early by underground as they call it,

where I am packed in next to a character wearing a blue and white scarf, which signifies that he is supporting Tottenham, and I ask him about the match and where he is going to stand, and in between pauses to shift his chewing gum from one side of his jaw to the other, he says he will stand down behind the goal at one particular end of the ground. And he says there is not such a good view of the football from this spot, but it is just the right place to get into a good fight. Well, personally, even in my state of health, if I never have to fight anything more frightening than this little runt, I do not think I need have any fears about being picked on. He is very much of a weed indeed. So I ask him who is he going to fight, and he states that he will be meeting up with a lot more runts and weeds and then they will get stuck in.

So it is evident that this character is more concerned about starting something than he is about the football.

Well, I get to the ground and there are millions of people round and about, so I find a policeman, and I address him as sergeant although he is nothing but a constable, and I tell him that one of my relations once gets the family a bad name by becoming a policeman, and he thinks this is very funny, and he knows about this relation of mine, and we become quite matey on account of it, and eventually he tells me where to find the most reputable ticket-touts, which is exactly what I want to know, because I do not fancy the idea of being suspected of being some stupid nit from the country and finding myself with a forged ticket palmed off on me. So before you can say 'Up the Arsenal', there I am with my ticket and inside the ground in a very nice position indeed.

It is a lovely field, but it is obvious it has to put up with some heavy hammering during the recent wet weather and, unless they rest it, they will never be able to hope for an early bite off it in the spring. There are covered stands right round the ground, and a great number of very bright lights, and everywhere there is an atmosphere of great expectancy on account of the desperate encounter which is about to take place.

It is not long before a delicate situation develops because there are Tottenham Hotspur supporters behind me, and Arsenal supporters in front of me. Now Tottenham Hotspur is a considerable mouthful for anybody to have to say at each time of asking, and so this team is known as the Spurs for short, but obviously it is impossible to abbreviate a name such as Arsenal and still remain on speaking terms with your neighbours. But this does not worry such neighbours as I have on this occasion, and what they call the Arsenal team and their supporters is not the sort of language you will normally expect to find in the parish church magazine.

However, I have a large amount of luck, because next to me there is an Irishman, and he only comes along to see a good game of football. So we are both neutral in this matter, and many stories are told about such characters on such occasions, but there is not enough space available for me to write about them here and now. Furthermore, my Irish friend turns out to be a rugby player in his time, so we get on famously, because, as I tell you before, I also have my moments in my younger days playing football egg-shaped. But I have the advantage over him, because in later life I also do a spot of refereeing, in the soccer code as they say, and I have a little card to prove that I pass an examination and am competent to blow the whistle or say 'play on' as I think fit.

As soon as the players come on to the field there is all hell let loose, for it so happens that this is the second leg of the League Cup and, when they meet a couple of weeks previously, Arsenal lead by one goal to nil, so they only have to keep a clean sheet in this encounter, and there are also some personal feuds to be settled from where they leave off the last time.

There is no shortage of the old needle whatsoever,

and within a few minutes the fists are flying. I do not know how the little runt and his mates are getting on in the crowd behind the goal, but if he is behaving any worse than some of the players, then he is behaving in a most disgraceful manner to be sure. It is customary for fighting to take place in such encounters towards the end of the game, but when it starts off right at the commencement of the ding-dong, then we are in for some real trouble. Or this is the way I am thinking, but it turns out that the referee is a Welshman, and he is bang on top of the job and he sorts them out to some tune.

In fact, one and all seem to be agreed that the referee is quite a good character, and this is most unusual on such occasions. Even so, there is so much kicking and hacking by some of the players, and also so much old argument and jaw, that you will understand why I say it is a very great demonstration of foot-and-mouth.

Just behind me there is a Spurs supporter, who must be the most empty-headed character ever to get into a football ground. Throughout the match he maintains a never-ending flow of vacuous inanities. The more usual 'get rid of it' or 'get stuck in' adjurations are interspersed with the comment 'goo' boo' which is presumably North London comment for 'good ball', and he immediately follows this with 'wuz a goo' boo', in case nobody believes him the first time. In the end he gets on the nerves of the Arsenal supporters, and they start shouting themselves but, of course, they are shouting for Arsenal. So I decide it is time to contribute to the occasion, and I start shouting for Swansea Town, and my Irish friend joins in the spirit of the thing and starts shouting for Tipperary. But as neither Swansea Town nor Tipperary are taking part in this foot-and-mouth demonstration, all the Arsenal and Spurs supporters think we are maybe a couple of nuts and have a good laugh about us instead of shouting insults at each other.

One of the principal Arsenal players is a character

called Ure, and I hope it is no disrespect to say that he has such a face as only his mother will ever be able to love, and he is marking a Spurs player by the name of England, who is a Welshman, which is confusing, and although this England is a tough character and looks very fierce, on account of having a moustache and gets his name written down in the referee's book, this Ure character really gives him his come-uppance. In fact, this Ure character is so good that before he finishes he even has the Spurs supporter behind me shouting — 'Goo' boo'. Wuz a goo' boo.'

Then it is all over and some knowledgeable characters explain to me that it is on account of the players earning so much that they behave in such an unruly manner. But I figure that the head bosses of each club will very soon be able to stop this nonsense if they so desire.

And I reckon if they are paying them so much money and still cannot get them to behave in a less unruly manner on the field, then the police do very well on the money they are getting to keep the damage amongst the spectators down to one stabbing. Especially as the one who is stabbed is behind the goal where they go to look for the trouble, whereas the players are supposed to be paid for playing football.

I am pleased to state, however, that as the whistle goes to signify it is all over this Ure goes straight up to Mr England to shake him by the hand, and other Spurs and Arsenal characters go round doing likewise. In fact the Arsenal players cannot now find anything else to do, so they run round kissing each other, and unless I see for myself how they stand up to the battering the Spurs players give them, I will consider they are a right lot of pansies.

So this explains all about the foot-and-mouth which is known as The Great Plague.

---

* FUW – Farmers' Union of Wales, a splinter movement from the National Farmers' Union of England and Wales, c. 1953.

Welsh Farm News, 1 February 1969

This is rather a sad tale this week. About a duck. He was shot, and we had him for dinner. What's more, he tasted good.

Time was when I was a bit of a shooting character, and I can still recall the red-letter day long years go when I had the good fortune to drop a couple of snipe with a right and a left, a feat which eluded many far better shots over a lifetime of effort and hope. It happened, I remember, when I graduated to a twelve bore from the twenty bore of my youth, and felt supremely confident with the greater spread of shot and apparently unlimited killing power. What's more, there were two witnesses, but both have now passed on and, I hope, are enjoying their sport in Elysian fields amongst far better types than some of the yobbos we see with guns today.

Yes, we enjoyed our shooting.

Somehow or other, though, I grew away from it. Perhaps it was something to do with the tender and mellowing influence of a girl with whom I fell in love, and she happened to think that there couldn't be all that much fun in destroying beautiful creatures just for the sheer hell of it.

Well, we've passed our silver wedding since then and most folks seem to reckon she's much too good for me and can't think what she could have seen in me in the first place, and naturally I continue to be influenced by one who is generally acknowledged to be such a kind and tender soul. In fact I often explain that it was only because of her kindness that she married me.

So that's how it is, and my bit of shooting nowadays doesn't amount to anything at all. But, mark you, although my interest in and love of the birds has increased over the years, I like to think I have retained a sense of proportion over the business. Certainly I do not condemn the shooting men who can still enjoy what I no longer find it in my heart to do.

Indeed, more than once in this column I have said that your true shooting men do more for real conservation than most of the so-called ornithologists and bird-ringers put together. Like the fishermen, they have a marvellous feeling for the lonely places, and the solitude and the wild things of the countryside.

I had been thinking particularly on these lines because I'd been reading a really delightful book entitled *A Fowler's World* by Ian Niall. In page after page of beautiful prose, the love of this sort of life was painted vividly by one who is content to shoot a couple of duck for his own plate and leave it go at that.

So convincing was the writing in places, I almost thought that maybe I shouldn't have given up the shooting after all. The floods were out. There were duck to be seen and studied and, for once in a while, I found myself wondering where would be the approach and the place to stand in which to have a chance of bagging one. Mr Niall is not optimistic for his chances when there is so much water about.

It was whilst I was in this frame of mind that word came that there was 'a nice big mallard drake' out in the field. Apparently this bird was on his own and could be approached to within twenty yards and would only then fly another thirty yards or so. Obviously there was something wrong with him. The weather hadn't been hard to weaken him, and the only thing we could think was that he was a bird wounded by somebody else's shot, or else that he was another victim of these hideous overhead power cables.

A wildfowler of my acquaintance tells me that these monstrosities have completely ruined his bend of the river where the duck now have to swing round so high that they are way beyond range even when they are to be seen at all.

Well, whatever this bird in our field was, he was certainly no ordinary mallard. So I telephoned a pal of mine who has forgotten more about birds than I'll ever know. Rather black it was, with a green bar on the wing and white wing tips. A white bar on the front of the neck and orange legs. It was too big to be any sort of scoter, and yet it didn't seem to be any one of the black geese. In the event it turned out to be five pounds in weight, and was identified as a cross between a muscovey and a mallard.

Over the telephone, however, my pal admitted to being completely bewildered. We agreed that to leave it where it was would be fatal. Night was approaching, and the foxes would ensure that he wouldn't be there in the morning. So it was agreed that, if we couldn't catch him, the only thing to do was to shoot him.

Three of us tried to catch him but, right from the start, it was obviously going to be a waste of time. He sailed high into the wind and over to the other side of the farm, so the gun it had to be.

The question of shooting a protected bird didn't really enter into it, for this one, being some sort of hybrid, appeared on no known list and, even if he had, I could honestly claim that I was doing no more than performing an act of mercy.

I dropped him coming quite fast downwind, for which I take no credit, except perhaps to say that easier shots have been missed, and I know about this because I've missed them myself. As I picked him up, however, with his handsome plumage soft to the touch, more beautiful than can readily be described, and a few drops of blood stained the wet winter grass, I knew in my heart that I wasn't really cut out to be a fowler.

A good friend of mine told me the following day that he'd gone out with the gun on Boxing Day. He'd intended going shooting with a neighbour but was too late finishing up in the morning. So rather than be done out of it altogether he walked round his own place with the gun, although he didn't expect to see anything.

He has a couple of useful ponds and he feeds the wild duck, but that has rather made it that he doesn't care to shoot them. But he saw a couple of rabbits and shot one, and he shot a pigeon. And he said he thinks he would perhaps have shot a snipe if he hadn't been wondering whether to re-seed the adjoining field or not, and he saw a grey squirrel without getting close enough to have a shot.

So, what with one thing and another, he enjoyed his morning. Then, just as he came back near the house, two geese came over low and close within easy range. And they looked lovely. Shoot?

'Of course not, man. Damn it all, there was plenty of turkey in the house, so we didn't need 'em for the pot, and if I'd shot one the other would have been left all alone and what sort of life is that?'

So you see, I have some very tidy friends as well as a kind-hearted wife. But when I explained to her about fowlers only really shooting for their own dinner, she said a pity Mr Niall didn't say in his book about who has to feather the so-and-so's.

Maybe after more than a quarter of a century my influence on her hasn't been a very good one.

Modern Farmer, September 1972

I am not, by any stretch of the imagination, either a radio or television fan. Shall we say I object to radio rather less than I do to television. Not that they don't have their uses. A quiet hour or so of cricket or good music when a chap is unable to get to the venue of the real thing can sometimes be most acceptable.

But I do wish people wouldn't take as gospel everything they hear and see on the radio or idiot's lantern. Particularly in the case of the weather forecasts. The world is full of characters who seem anxious to make a living, and I can't ever remember having heard or read that there is any law against this.

But while they may be worth every penny of what they are paid to discourse with great erudition on topics various, I do so wish that others would remember that these types are but mere humans and are therefore fallible. Like the rest of us, they could be right and they could be wrong.

All this is all right as far as it goes, but if there is one thing that really drives me round the twist about the whole foolish circus, it is the way in which so many other sensible characters, who ought to know better, seem to swallow, hook, line and sinker, whatever the weather forecast says.

Not that I'm against having a weather forecast. Nor am I agin those who make the forecast or those who read it out. We all have to live. When you look at some of them mind, you wonder why, but that's another story.

What I am really agin is the way mankind has been conditioned into thinking that it's all the gospel truth. And anybody who thinks that the long range forecast is anything more than another big belly laugh really needs his head reading. It's the ordinary forecast I have in mind just now.

Throughout the countryside are many ancient

characters who are extremely weatherwise and can usually give you a fair idea of what is going to happen. They're not always right any more than the man on the goggle box, but their opinion is usually worth having, and I'm never averse to asking for it.

They know the implications of a ring round the moon, and recognise a watery sun. They are wise in the matter of cloud formation, and the height and speed of the clouds. They know when the sound is up or down, when distant hills are too close, or if it is looking too black over Bill's mother's.

Sometimes they are suddenly troubled with the screws, and the ducks quack loud, the pigs are restless, the leaves on the trees turn every which way, rooks take to gliding in their flight, dogs take to chewing grass, which is maybe not always because they have worms, and the weatherwise ancients know what to expect. They have the time to observe such happenings, and the experience to interpret their portent.

How, then, man's faith in humanity is shattered when you ask such characters what the weather is going to do, and they start off by saying, 'The forecast says . . .'

And then I have to point out to them that I'm not interested in what the forecast says, and even if I were, I could listen to it for myself. This is a sound basis for an interesting discussion on how stupid some of the town folks are, and how little the forecasters know and, no, the ancient doesn't think there will be much rain in it.

And this can always bring relief to a troubled soul who has a field of hay down and happens to have been listening to the wrong forecast. But at the rate we're going, some of them will soon have become so obsessed by what the forecast says that there will be nobody left who is willing to think and work it out for himself.

Come to think of it, if any political party will take as an election plank a pledge to get rid of the weather forecasts I'll give 'em a vote.

Modern Farmer, October 1972

The Bunny-puzzle

To me, at any rate, there seemed something rather odd about the announcement by the Ministry of Agriculture that the whole of the country had been designated a rabbit clearance area with the exception of the City of London, the Isles of Scilly and Skokholm Island.

There's probably a great deal of sense in it somewhere, but that still doesn't prevent it seeming odd to me. Maybe it's because I'm odd.

Why, now, should the City of London be excluded? Is it because there are no rabbits there, or because somebody is afraid that to include the Metropolis might be misinterpreted as meaning that there was to be an all-out effort to exterminate pests frequenting the joint?

I suppose there are plenty of pests there still. But I always said at the time that the Government of the day were worth at least one vote and another chance for the way they cleared some of them off the streets after old Wolfenden* had made his report.

I know the effect was merely to drive them underground, but it's worth mentioning because the rabbits also seem to have changed their habits and now spend a fair bit of time above ground, whereas previously they used to get up to their tricks underground where nobody could see what they were doing, but everybody had a pretty good idea from the self-evident results.

I also said that the Government of the day were worth at least one vote and another chance for the way in which they abolished the gin-trap. Certainly this bit of legislation was the greatest single contribution to controlling the rabbit problem and one which ensured that rabbits need never again become too numerous.

However, we were talking about underground

activities. There are those who believe that rabbits are now loath to go underground as in days of yore because they know that they would be easier victims for the stoats and weasels, and in Wales at any rate, the polecats, which are all very much on the increase since the demise of the gin-trap. I subscribe to that view myself.

For what it may be worth, and I don't think it is very much, there are also those who think the rabbits do not seem so keen on going underground for fear of picking up the fleas which are the carriers of myxomatosis.

And this brings us to the question of why Skokholm should be excluded. The idea seems to be that the rabbits on Skokholm cannot get myxomatosis because they have been found, for some reason or other, to be incapable of supporting a flea.

So, if the fleas cannot live on the rabbit, it cannot make an incision into the skin and that is why the rabbit does not get myxomatosis.

Therefore this island is not included in the order because it is a great thing to have such places to carry out all sorts of experiments for an unsuspecting but doubtlessly grateful nation.

Well, then, we may ask, why do they exclude the neighbouring island of Skomer which is held by the same outfit and where the rabbits can and do get myxomatosis because the dirty little perishers have fleas?

The fact that nobody will bother about this is neither here nor there, except that it makes the law an ass from the word 'go'. And this doesn't matter either because everybody knows that the law is an ass anyway.

So we are left with the Isles of Scilly. And between you and me, but don't tell anyone else, because I wouldn't want it to get round and for everybody to know about it, I haven't a clue as to what is so particular and peculiar about the Isles of Scilly.

Wherefore I can only assume that the Tory Government wouldn't want people to run away with the idea that they would like to exterminate that nice Mr. Wilson**.

Ah, well, we have to live and let live, don't we? But when I look at some on 'em I wonders why. I just wonders.

* Lord Wolfenden chaired the committee appointed to look, amongst other things, into the way prostitutes plied their trade on the streets. His report was published in 1957.
** Harold Wilson, a little man, smooth-talking Prime Minister, and a stranger to the truth. He had a holiday home in the Isles of Scilly.

Modern Farmer, June 1973

Not So Clever, Look You

How difficult are the times in which we live. By almost every post news comes of trials and tribulations.

Livestock worrying by dogs is the least of the problems, serious though it is.

There is farm safety, and the possible hazards from linkage-mounted diggers and loaders, there is swayback in lambs, nematodirus, liver fluke, swine vesicular disease and warble-fly, to say nothing of mastitis, and periods of high fire risk in trees.

Endless hand-outs have been issued on these subjects, as well as on inflation and the ravages of the grey squirrel.

It is mention of the grey squirrel, however, which brings to mind the greatest bit of nonsense to have been heard for some time, and we are not particularly proud of the fact that it has emanated from Wales.

The grey squirrel is a great menace, which is a fact which is well-known to one and all. And if it's known to one and all then you can take it from me that includes just about everybody.

The current slogan is 'Plant a Tree in '73.'

Next comes 'Plant some more in '74.'

And after that, if they can't do something about the grey squirrels, it will be 'See if they're alive in '75.'

Well, it seems that some enterprising types have been experimenting with hormone baits for grey squirrels which would have the effect of discouraging the little perishers from breeding.

A sort of do-it-yourself contraceptive outfit for these lower species. It was only a short step to the suggestion that it would be a great boon if only the scientific characters could think up the same sort of stunt for the rabbits.

Why, I wonder, should so many people be getting worked up about the rabbit?

The disappearance of the gin-trap meant that the rabbit need never again be the national menace it had become in the pre-myxomatosis years.

Apart from the fact that the gin-trap 'swarmed' the rabbits by leaving behind a very high proportion of does to bucks, the fact that the gin-trap is no longer in use means that the stoats, weasels and polecats are once again coming back in sufficient numbers to help to take care of any excessive rabbit population.

The odd day's ferreting or a few hours 'lamping' by night are all that is needed to keep the position under control.

Modern Farmer, **December 1973**

There are times in life when I sit and ponder and always come to the same apparently inescapable conclusion that, with all its defects and shortcomings, and in spite of all its detractors say about it, education is a great thing.

It doesn't only enable you to understand decimal money and work out VAT. I am thinking in particular about English as she is spoke.

Maybe I have a complex about this, but have you noticed how many people can find you a complex these days? Everything is a complex. You can't hear a news bulletin on the goggle-box or pick up a paper without reading about a complex.

Half the time they are more likely to be talking about a simple, but that doesn't seem to deter them. If it's only a couple of buildings near a farmhouse, it's now a complex. But not to worry. This, too, like suffering, will pass. Joy always cometh in the morning. Hopefully.

Whilst we're on the subject, can we, at this moment in time, think of some of the others? Admittedly things don't seem to be as pragmatic as they once were, but the idiot usage of other expressions also seems to be escalating.

Right across the board the media helps to create the image and seems to be intent on doing just that. What the object of the exercise is I am not quite sure. Some of them may be just another lot of male chauvinist pigs but, at the end of the day, they don't by and large appear to be very meaningful as such.

I myself, speaking personally as an individual, think we could do with a teach-in on this subject. Sometimes it makes me get very uptight and of the opinion that we could do with a send-up.

We have in fact come a long way from the days when, as farmers, we were being exhorted to minimise the throughput in order to maximise the output, although that was not the co-efficient of the ratio related to their linear programming aimed at realising the full potential.

What one feels about this sort of thing, however, is that one has to be objective, and if one is not wanting to be merely destructive, then one simply has to be constructive and, at the same time, one has to be particularly careful to let one know to which one one is referring, otherwise one will find oneself in one hell of an old ding-dong.

The point in mentioning this is because of the integrated management options which must always be left open in the event of a balanced policy contingency.

Obviously, with the price of feeding stuffs being what it is this winter all along the western seaboard, and Heath backing up Godber on standing firm over the price of milk, there is no point as I see it in putting our shoulders to the wheel and leaving no stone unturned in our determination to explore every avenue.

The total reciprocal concept must never at any one moment in time be allowed to offset the integration of a functional incremental projection, otherwise both the responsive digital capability and the parallel organisational flexibility can never be expected to achieve a compatible logistical outcome.

We were doing our own thing here the other day when I happened to mention that the advice most recently given to me was to guard against transitional mobility.

I asked my teenage son, who has just been doing A level English, what this really means, and he said, 'All it means is don't let the buggers move you sideways.'

'Ah,' said I. 'As we used to say in our younger days, '*nil illegitimae carborundum*', which, as everybody knows, means, 'don't let the bastards grind you down'.' That is why I said that bit at the beginning about education. Period. End of story.

Private Ear, July 1974

Luck of the Draw
by Clogghead

Good customers they may have been. But the new
manager had a point. And he also had a job to do.
There were thousands of pounds on the books
outstanding and the pressure was on from all sides.

The first letter was very civil, due attention to and
requested the favour of. A few of the more gentlemanly
types responded, but the results were not spectacular.

The follow-up letter, however, was rather more to
the point with a distinct impression of iron somewhere
hid beneath the velvet exterior of the glove of the hand
which wrote it.

The results were gratifying but left the hard core
unimpressed and unmoved. And this led to the
penultimate letter which bordered on the offensive as
well as the starkly terrifying. Only the most hardened
cases remained obdurate in the face of it and were
clearly beyond the pale. Being beyond hope, less than
the dust and of no further consequence, their names
were listed for throwing to the not-so-tender mercies of
the legal eagles.

At this point the Rep said yes, that's all well and
good, but not that one. After all was said and done he
had the job of calling on him every month, and he
wasn't a bad sort anyway and he'd been a customer for
forty years and always paid up in the end and maybe
paid a bit of something on account when the case was
really explained to him. So the manager said that was
as maybe and those were the orders from above and it
was all the same to him. So the Rep, who had a nagging
wife and hungry children, said well let him just call on
this character first and see what a bit of gentle coaxing
might do and the manager said all right then, twenty-

four hours and no more.

Well, when the Rep gets to the farm the farmer says come in very friendly and have a cup of tea, and then the Rep gets round to the subject of the account and the farmer says come out here and leads the Rep into the back kitchen. And there the Rep can see an old-fashioned end-over butter churn. And the farmer says he supposes the Rep knows what that is and the Rep, who once did a day release course at a farm institute, says yes that is an old-fashioned end-over butter churn.

'That's right,' says the farmer, 'and now I'll tell you what I uses it for. Every month when the milk cheque comes I takes all the bills and puts 'em in the churn and gives it a fair old swish round to mix 'em all up and then I pulls 'em out one by one and pays 'em off until the milk cheque have all gone. Then I puts the rest of 'em on one side until the next milk cheque comes and then I starts all over again. And I knows your lot haven't been very lucky in the draw just lately. But you go back and tell that new man of yours that any more cheek from him or many more letters like the last one he sent here and your name won't even go into the bloody churn.'

Modern Farmer, Vol. 12 No: 4 1974

Now it came to pass that there was great trouble in the land, and there were Cons and Labs and Libs, wherefore did Ted and Harold and Jeremy* seek to find favour in the sight of the people.

And there had been a time of great contentment throughout the land forasmuch as a decree had gone forth that no picture should appear upon the goggle after a certain hour.

But when it became known that Ted and Harold and Jeremy sought to find favour in the sight of the people, a new decree went forth so that Ted and Harold, and Jeremy and many of those that were with them, should appear upon the goggle at all times.

And when they appeared not upon the goggle there were those who came with arrows and dots and many symbols of great mystery, and these were the opinion polls.

And when there were no opinion polls to be spoken of upon the goggle there came other arrows and dots and symbols, and this was the long-range weather forecast.

And when those who spake of such matters said it would rain it rained not, likewise when they said the sun would shine it shone not.

But when they said it would freeze and that snow would fall, then of a surety the sun would shine so that there was great confusion.

Now for many moons the shepherds and humble men who tilled the soil had been exhorted by the leaders of the people to grow much food, which was known as expansion and for which there would be great reward.

But there were many in the land who were known as cartoonists, and they depicted the shepherds and humble men as being like unto a donkey that pursueth a carrot on the end of a stick, inasmuch as the donkey shall move forward so also shall the carrot remain beyond their reach at all times.

Wherefore did the shepherds and humble men speak of Ted and Harold and Jeremy and say: 'They are scurvy fellows.'

Thus did Ted and Harold and Jeremy and all the Cons and the Labs and the Libs go through the land and appear upon the goggle in order that they might find favour in the sight of the people and receive a mandate.

But the people heeded not their words and promises, saying: 'Of a surety, have we not heard all this before?'

And when the day came that the people should speak with one voice they lifted up their voices in unison and said get stuffed, which was after the manner of speaking of those times, and Ted and Harold and Jeremy received not a mandate.

Wherefore were the opinion polls seen as matters of great foolishness which were no more reliable than computers or babies' bottoms in former times, for always it had been the custom for men to speak of certain matters as being no more reliable than certain other matters.

And it had been known throughout the ages, and handed down by word of mouth, that nothing could be any less reliable than a baby's bottom until the opinion polls and politicians' promises and computers and the long range weather forecast.

Wherefore did Harold come to be pragmatic in all things, and there was great trouble in the land.

---

* Ted Heath, Harold Wilson, Jeremy Thorpe. Leaders of the Tory, Labour and Liberal parties respectively, not respectably. There was nothing particularly respectable about any of them.

British Farmer and Stockbreeder, 25 June 1977

Getting at the roots of agriculture

To get in was easy enough, apart from a bit of a traffic jam and that. But to get out was a different matter.

As one, therefore, who does not take kindly to having to admit defeat, Jones Co-op Management Committee is determined to try again this year.

Last year he went with the intention of looking at the most recent improvements to the mobile sheep-handling pens and came away with a pair of guaranteed non-run fully-fashioned lady's stockings, a non-stick frying pan, a self-propelling reversible ever-sharp knife, a fountain pen that would write under water, and he had placed an order for a swimming pool. It was hot for the time of year you may remember.

He had also signed bankers' orders for membership of the AA, the British Field Sports Society, the League against Cruel Sports, and the Society for the Preservation of the Pot-bellied Warthog. He was not very well at the time and explained to the gentleman that he had signed a banker's order in favour of the R.A.S.E. the year before.

Jones CMC had also had an altercation with a man with a beard and a small tent, outside of which was a table covered with leaflets, who wanted to save the soul of Jones from everlasting damnation. Jones, a lifelong member of Zion and Hebron Reformed Methodists Combined, told him to pray for the soul of John Silkin. Cutting tongue Jones has, with a nice turn of phrase. He also told him there was a taxidermist with a stand in the next avenue. And he knew about that because he'd been down that avenue as well.

What happened was that Jones got lost when all he was trying to do was to go home. 'Tis a hard thing, friends, when all you want in life is to go home and the hand of fate has conspired with the Royal Organisation itself to make it impossible.

He had learned his lesson about the vast and crowded car park the hard way the year before, when he had found his way back to it, but hadn't made a note of his bearings in the morning. So he had decided to go back in for an hour or two until the ranks had thinned out somewhat. They had explained the rule about no readmission, and that's when he had signed the banker's order for membership. Last year, therefore, he carried a pocket compass with him and took his bearings in between a tree which had been struck with Dutch elm disease and a Rolls Royce flying a standard incorporating a red dragon rampant.

All of this, however, proved to be of no use when he tried to get out. Eventually he hove to alongside a big board which said quite clearly, with an arrow to explain it in even more detail, 'You Are By Here.' Jones, however, did not want to be by here. He wanted to be by there. So he lurched along to the next board and still found he was by here. At six more boards he was till by here, and all he had done in the meantime was to buy the frying pan and stockings and join a few good societies, because being on the Co-op Management Committee he knew that must be a good thing to do.

Then he saw this gentleman with a bowler hat and a pin-striped suit and a badge as big as a manhole cover, so he asked him how to get out. Obviously taken aback at the thought of anybody wanting to get out of the place, the character with the bowler hat, showing a marked flair for public relations, said, 'I say, old chap, my name's Cad Hyphen Wallader. Do come in and have a drink and let's see if we can discuss this thing reasonably. Lord Fanshaw is terribly keen on this sort of thing, you know. Frightfully keen. Has some marvellous ideas about it. Absolutely must keep in touch with the members at the grass roots and all that jazz. Don't you agree the grass roots are most terribly important, old chap?'

When Lord Fanshaw was located, however, he was in a rare old predicament.

'Damned fellow' he said. 'Only appointed to the judges' list last year and there he is in the main ring wearing a straw hat and the Royal Personage due any minute.'

'I quite agree with you, Snooky, old chap. Knew it would lead to trouble as soon as MCC allowed members to watch without jackets. Hot weather be damned. They'll be taking their ties off next.'

They each called one more drink apiece for Jones before dashing off to take up the matter with the senior steward concerning the judge without a bowler hat, and exhorted Jones to look in any old time because they were terribly keen to keep in touch with the grass roots, and Jones hadn't even told them he was a member of the Co-op Management Committee.

So there it is. He got home in the end and he's going again this year. What's more he's going to wear his bowler hat. The one he bought for the day when they inducted him as a deacon at Zion and Hebron Reformed Methodists Combined.

First thing he's going to do is look out his old friends Hyphen and Snooky so that he can keep in touch with the grass roots. As a member of the Co-op Management Committee it's the least he can do and that way, he reckons, they can all keep up with the Joneses.

Stock Press [Ciba Geigy], 1977

The instructions on the label
by Clogghead

Officious type he was. This inseminator. Officious. And
fussy with it. Not the type in fact to go down at all well
with the character of whom I wish to tell you.

Now this character – not the inseminator, but the
character of whom I wish to tell you – was a farmer.
What is known as a small farmer. There again, to be
explicit and to avoid confusion, not wishing to imply
that he only stood about five feet two inches before
going metric, which he wouldn't have been the type to
do anyway. I mean that he was a small farmer insofar
as he only had about a dozen cows.

Now this small farmer, whenever he had a cow to be
inseminated, would get the cow in and, to make life
easier for himself and to keep the cow happy, would
get another cow in with her and tie them up alongside
each other in the cowshed and then go off and leave
them because he would usually have other duties to
attend to like digging graves or catching rabbits, since
nobody can figure on earning a living waiting for the
inseminator to call in between milking a dozen cows
twice a day.

So, what with one thing and another, the
inseminator couldn't remember when he had last set
eyes on this small farmer until one day he came in
answer to the call, and there was the farmer in the
farmyard and the two cows in the cowshed and the
scene is set for that of which I shall now proceed to
speak.

You will remember that this inseminator is a very
officious type, and he points out to the farmer that,
when he has two cows in the shed, and is not there to
identify them personally and to vouch for their good

character and condition and state of health generally, then it is provided for in the rules that he must have some identification mark upon them, like a label on the tail or some such.

'Because,' says this inseminator, 'how am I to know which cow is in season, and wouldn't you be the first so-and-so to kick up a fuss if I inseminated the wrong one? And what is more,' says the inseminator, who is now warming to his theme, it also says in the rules that you must provide a clean towel and a bar of soap and some warm water, but whenever I come here what do I find? Not a damn thing', says the inseminator, because there are people like that in life who love answering their own questions, which is maybe why they ask them.

'So, in future,' concludes the inseminator, 'let's have things right, and now we know where we stand.'

Well, of course, with the farmer being a grave-digger and that, and therefore a very respectful type, he touches his cap and says yes sir, of course sir, and three bags full sir, and that concludes the matter and he will be quite sure to attend to that small thing.

Sure enough, the next time the call comes, the inseminator pulls up in his car, gets out, looks into the cowshed, and there are two cows tied up, and the one has an auctioneer's ticket stuck on her tail-head. And the inseminator smiles, and then he sees a towel hanging up on a nail behind the door, a pan of warm water and a bar of soap alongside it. And the inseminator smiles some more and looks as happy as a dog with two lamp-posts.

Then he goes back to the boot of the car, gets his oilskin bib-and-tucker on, into the aluminium chest, tube between his teeth and back into the cowshed. Left hand well forward in the excavating action, left arm straight and chin well down like they do in Pot Black. Then he sees what is on the label – 'Not this one – the other one.'

Private Ear, July 1977

Fate Worse than Death
by Clogghead

A warm, sensuous breeze slipped through the strong standing wheat. The flag was broad and clean and the future was full of promise.

In early summer everything had gone well. For days after the nozzles had passed overhead with their deadly sprays the weather had remained warm and dry. Now there was not a weed to be seen.

As the ear emerged there was one full-bodied grain who fancied her chances more than all the others, and as the summer advanced she began to develop ideas of her own.

From what she saw of the life being led by the partridges, male and female, she could hardly be blamed for putting two and two together and thinking how beautiful the world could be. They had their nest right there beneath her and so she could hardly help seeing all that was going on. Well, she had to turn her head just a little, but my goodness what a carry on it was and my goodness dearie-me.

There were a couple of rabbits as well who were no better than they ought to be and the things they got up to would have rated a couple of pages in the glossy magazines.

Nobody had told her anything of the facts of life or the sort of things a grain of wheat ought to know. But when she could see what was going on around her, and felt the warm, sensuous breeze stirring her whole being, well then, so what.

It was just at that time that she caught the eye of a 'sport' across the way. He nodded at her and she went all coy and blushed, and then she nodded back at him. After that their affair just blossomed. Not that there

155

was anything that either of them could do about it just then for they always seemed to be the regular four inches apart. Occasionally a mischievous stray breeze would throw them momentarily closer together and she thrilled at his touch. It made her build plans for the future with even greater fervency.

What a time they would have. Just like the partridges and the rabbits, bringing into the world a whole new race of sports.

Ha, cruel fate. Hard world that it is.

It was just then that the combine harvester was turned loose to devour all before it into its insatiable mouth. What was a poor grain of wheat in face of such as this?

A horrible blackness was suddenly upon her. Wither or which way she went she knew not. Round and round, backwards and forwards. Above and below, up and down. Oh, hideous doubt. What unspeakable horror was this?

At last the day dawned clear and bright. Fearfully she looked around her. Suddenly the awful truth impinged itself upon her consciousness. She was in a loaf of whole wheat bread on a shelf in the window of a baker's shop.

With one last despairing sob she cried: 'Oh, my God! I've been reaped.'

Private Ear, September 1978

'Nice weather, Mr. Jones'
by Clogghead

He had never done any showing himself, but he knew all about it, because he hadn't missed a show in the district since he couldn't remember when. And the one thing that always struck him was the consistently poor standard of the stock. Especially the stock which won.

He could hardly remember a show when the champion hadn't been inferior to something he had at home.

Now it is one thing for a character to recognize that he has something at home which is better than the champion, and it is a very comforting thought indeed for a character to recognize such. But when a character is not content with this but has to go into the beer tent afterwards and open his big mouth and proclaim to anybody willing to listen that he has something at home which would make the champion look like a candidate for the next load for the knacker's yard, then other characters are apt to ask is it not time that they had a chance to have a look at this very good stock.

So there it is and that's the way it goes, and in the end this character opens his big mouth so wide and so often that he just about convinces himself that all he has to do is collect the winner's ticket. And in the spring he has one ewe with a single lamb, which is a ram lamb at that, and he reckons it is just about as good a lamb as he ever has, which means it is a very good lamb indeed and then some.

Wherefore and therefore what this character does is to give this very special ram lamb the treatment from the word go and makes no small investment in combs and brushes and one thing and another, and the feed is right and he also gets a nice cotton halter, and the ram lamb learns to walk a real masterpiece.

By the day of the show he knows that the winning ticket is as good as his and all he has to do is to collect it, but first of all, of course, he will have to go through the formality of going into the ring for the judge to have a look before saying what a very fine ram lamb to be sure and have much pleasure in telling the steward to give him the winning ticket.

Well, what happens then is that the steward comes along to the pens and says to all the characters with ram lambs please to bring them into the judging ring and they can hardly be such ram lambs as are due for the knacker's yard because this character's ram lamb is about the only lamb the judge doesn't seem to notice. In fact, not only is he not anywhere in the frame, but the judge does not as much as say 'Thank-you-for-coming.'

So there is this character on his way back to the stock pens and leading his ram lamb, and feeling very dejected and disheartened, when who should come along but the vicar who says, 'Nice weather, Mr. Jones.'

And this character says, 'Not yet, vicar, but wait till I get the bugger home.'

Stock Press [Ciba Geigy], November 1979

First catch your sheep
by Clogghead

First of all, Mrs. Beeton used to say, you catch your hare and then you cook it.

Well, maybe it's not a bad order for your priorities at that. Certainly the farmer would seem to have thought so, for he decided to get his sheep in first of all and then to dip them. Not that he had been reading Mrs. Beeton. He had previously picked up that tip at an ADAS* demonstration. They're very good like that in explaining to the likes of thee and me that you cannot possibly dip your sheep until you have caught them. So the farmer decided to catch his sheep.

The way he reckoned to catch them was in his sheep-handling pen. This was another good idea he had picked up somewhere from somebody. Probably his father or grandfather or somebody like that.

Unfortunately, nobody had ever told him how to get his sheep in without the help of his sheepdog. And this particular day his dog had taken it in his head to go off because there was a bitch in heat somewhere and it is well known to one and all that, even to a sheepdog, not even chasing sheep is half as exiting as the prospect of a bitch in heat.

Wherefore and therefore, and not to make a long story even longer, the farmer had to chase his own sheep on account of being all on his lonesome that day. And for a couple of hours he ran and chased and damned and blasted and a lot more awful words besides, in addition to casting serious doubts upon the sheep's ancestry and parentage, but, after two hours of sweat and fury he was no nearer to getting the sheep in than when he started. They were mountain sheep, of course.

It was just at this point, or moment in time, as characters say these days when they don't know how to speak proper, that the farmer espied a city gent walking up across the field towards him. Bowler hat, pin-stripe trousers, brief case, the lot. Right down to his patent leather shoes.

He was, he told the farmer, a civil servant, and he had been advised to go out into the country for some fresh air and exercise and one thing and another, including a change on account of his being on the verge of a nervous breakdown because he had been overworking filling in too many forms and that, and in fact during the previous week he had been called upon to make a decision, which had been the last straw. So here he was and could the farmer give him something to do.

Well, of course, the farmer was anxious to dip his sheep because the man at the demonstration had said this was a good thing to do, so he says to the civil servant by all means, if it would help him to get over his nervous breakdown, just go and round up the sheep and put them in that there sheep-handling pen.

So the farmer went off to the house to have his bit of bread and cheese and put his aching feet up and shut his eyes for ten minutes and, when he got back to the field, there was the civil servant sweating more than somewhat in his shirt-sleeves and with a layer of dust on his patent leather shoes, but with the two hundred mountain ewes all tucked away nicely, thank you, in the sheep-handling pen.

Well, of course, the farmer was greatly amazed at this spectacle. Even more amazed was he when he went up to the pen and there, lying down in the middle of the sheep, was a hare. Like the civil servant, the hare, too, was panting more than somewhat, with his long ears flat down on his back, and presenting a very defeated and dispirited picture to be sure.

'Well look at that,' said the farmer. 'That's a hare. I would never have believed it. A hare!'

'I don't know what it is,' said the civil servant, 'but that bugger gave me more trouble than the other two hundred put together.'

---

* ADAS: Agriculture Development and Advisory Service

Stock Press, **April 1980**

'Let us spray, said the parson'
by Clogghead

Well, as the twin bull calf said to the cow, 'Pass de udder udder to my udder brudder mudder.'

To put it another way, and it is Shakespeare who is credited with having said it first, 'There are more ways of killing a cat than stuffing it with cream.'

This is brought to mind by two items currently in the news. Firstly, there is the case of the lady in Sussex who wants to put a brake on the increase of unwanted cats all over the place, and has not only suggested putting cats on the pill, but is willing to provide pills for same. The only weakness in the scheme is that the people who couldn't care less will not bother to give the pills to their cats anyway.

There is always a snag somewhere, like there has been in the other story in the news, where they had a plague of rats on a South African island. So they introduced some cats. Now they are overrun with cats, which have not bothered with the rats, but have been slaughtering all the seabirds.

We had, and still have, a plague of cats round here, although at one time we thought we had found the answer. We traced most of the trouble to one particular ginger Tom.

Just at that time a rather enterprising character had heard about the new Ciba Geigy spray for teats. So he got to work and developed a most powerful and potent anaesthetic packed in a highly compressed sprayer which was deadly from anything up to ten yards or maybe more if the aim was true. He then explained that there would be no need to catch the ginger Tom and put his head in a jug. One well aimed jet from this highly compressed sprayer of his most powerful and potent spray would put the ginger Tom out of the copulation stakes for life. The same principle exactly as in the milking parlour. No dipping. Just spray.

It seemed like a good idea, so an ad hoc meeting of the standing joint committee of the parish council was called in situ. The parson is a co-opted member. We have a proper respect for the Cloth, and it is nice to have the parson's blessing on whatever the activity may be in which we are currently involved. Having heard the facts of the case, along with the proposal, the parson said, 'Let us spray.'

Well, they caught him all right [ginger Tom that is, not the vicar] up there on top of the fence. The jet came from behind and underneath, and the days of bliss for ginger Tom were over for ever.

There is, however, always a snag.

Everything went well for a long time. No unwanted kittens. No feline carousels with the accompanying midnight yowling. All was peace. Success had been achieved. Or so it seemed. Then all hell was let loose once again with kittens all over the place.

We called in our phantom sprayer and he went out on an exploratory tour. It was a lovely moonlight night, and there was ginger Tom, sitting on the lawn in the moonlight, with about twenty virile young Toms, sitting in a semi-circle round him, and hanging on his every word.   Included in his advice was how to keep their business ends away from the destruction of the lethal spray.

And the moral of the story is, if you can't do the job yourself, set up as a consultant.

Modern Farmer, October 1981

Backs to the land

Well, this farmer called and said that as long as we had a sack of potatoes there would be no problems, and he was pretty sure he knew enough about it now to be able to do the job himself – and in any case he was quite willing to try. So maybe I should explain.

Do you have any idea what happens when the lady of the house is confined to bed with back trouble? You know the idea. Slipped-disc business.

Progress is steady, but not nearly as spectacular as well-wishers think it should be. So staying on your back in bed with a board under the mattress for a fortnight is no sort of answer at all.

With one voice they tell you that they know a man.

The only problem is that it's not the same man. They each know a different man and *their* man is the tops.

One has the walls lined with framed certificates about the nature and good-health societies to which he belongs. Somewhat idiosyncratic, he treats the patient with a cigarette in his mouth. I don't know which of the health societies promotes this ploy, but it is apparently a trifle disconcerting when the ash drops on the vertebrae.

Another highly recommended chap has the patient strip off in a cold room and insists on carrying out the treatment on a cold slab. His rival just down the road has the patient in what virtually amounts to a sweat-box. Different treatment altogether.

Only this afternoon I heard from a lady whose husband, an inoffensive little man of five feet six inches, went to one joint where they pulled him about and stretched him to such purpose that when he came out he felt about six-feet-two. On re-reading this sentence I think maybe I should not have used the word joint in that context.

In contrast is one whose father taught him his trade by getting him to keep the cogwheel of a watch in his pocket and, without looking, count the number of cogs. I should think that when he has cured all the backs that need curing he'll be a likely recruit for anybody wanting a strong-room door to be opened on the quiet.

A more spectacular regimen is used by a regular sufferer I know who does not have time to go to an osteopath, and indeed cannot even afford it. When her back gives trouble she lies on the floor, face down, and her husband runs up and down it. 'Of course,' she told me, 'my husband is not as heavy as I am.'

But to return to the farmer who told us he could do the job himself with the aid of a sack of spuds. He was once in terrible pain and, having tried maybe a dozen or more of these manipulative characters, in desperation he went to the doctor.

The doctor sent him straight home to bed, not to move, and also prescribed some tablets. Working on the theory that if one tablet would do him good, two would do him twice as much good, he took two. Next thing he knew he was as high as a kite and, being a good Welshman, singing to the top of his voice.

Just then one of his neighbours called in and, of course, *he* knew a man. So off they went in the car way up into the hills in the bow-and-arrow country, and there they found this character, six-feet-five in his stocking-feet – and he was in his stocking-feet at the time, and hadn't shaved for a fortnight.

Unlike the chap with the cog out of the watch, he had learned his trade by manipulating the vertebrae of dogs' skeletons. This is known as a working knowledge. So he took the patient, who was still too high to know what he was doing, and should probably never have been allowed out without his Mammy in the first place, and led him over to the back of a farm wagon with a sack of potatoes on it.

Then he said for the patient to put his arms round the sack of potatoes and, with that, in went the big man's fist into the small of his back, and it was a good job he was still as high as a kite otherwise he doesn't know what he would have done.

'Unfortunately,' he said, 'I cannot remember the name of the tablets, but any time missus feels like embracing a sack of potatoes on the back of a wagon, I can show you exactly what to do.'

Being a courteous type by nature, I said we would wait until we had the names of some more men and then we would make our choice.

Do *you* happen to know a man by any chance? Yes, we already have a sack of potatoes, but thank you for the offer nevertheless.

Stock Press, **February 1982**

So . . . mind your own business!
by Clogghead

Well, this chap had a funny way with him, if he didn't want to answer a question, of saying it was the same as the bees and the sheep. So this other chap started making enquiries about the bees and the sheep, and what did this first chap mean, and then, when the other chap found out, he wasn't any wiser anyway.

What it was, this dealer turned up at the mart every week, and always bought all the screws that were going. All the old screw cows and even screw sheep. Old, broken-mouthed ewes, with hardly any wool, and gone in the udder, would always be knocked down to him.

Of course, this was a time just after the war, when nobody knew quite what was what, and a different chap altogether asked this dealer what the idea was. All these old screws, even old broken-mouthed ewes, with hardly any wool, and gone in the udder, and what on earth was the dealer doing with them? Were they going into manufacture, knackers yard, or black market for tasty pies, and how on earth could he make any money out of them?

So that was when the dealer told this different chap altogether about the bees and the sheep. It was also at a time when injecting to improve growth-rate was in its infancy, and the story was that, in some experiment or other, some outfit had got off to a wonderful start with some spectacular results.

And the dealer said that he had a brother who had just come back from Australia, and that this brother of his had been telling them about some strange things that had been happening out there. In fact, the dealer's brother had said, there were some places in the wild,

167

remote interior of Australia, where the most unusual things sometimes happened. Sometimes, he said, things would start to grow and grow very fast and very big indeed in this wild and remote part of Australia, and sometimes even the bees would grow as big as sheep. Well, of course, for bees to grow as big as sheep they would have to be very big bees indeed.

So, unable to contain his curiosity any longer, this chap said to the dealer, 'What, as big as sheep? Whichever way did they get into the hive?'

'Ah, well now,' said the dealer, 'that's their business.'

---

21 June 1956

He took the bus home and his mother made him take it back.

Farming Wales, January 1984

Do you, by any chance, know anything about bees?

If you don't, you're in good company, for neither do I, and I hope and trust you will take my word for it.

On the other hand, if you do happen to know anything about bees, there will be no need for you to take my word for it that I do not know anything about them, because it will very soon become evident, since I propose to write about them.

Not that there is any law against characters writing or speaking about things about which they know nothing, and that is why there is such great foolishness being written and spoken here and there and round and about generally.

In fact, it makes me think that, as we have so many laws, maybe there would be no harm in having one more law to prevent characters writing and speaking about things of which they know nothing, and then we could have a bit of peace and quiet about the place generally and save some paper which is now being wasted.

However, like I said, there is no law against it, and so I am going to write about bees.

Of course, I do not want to write about bees as such, to use a phrase much loved by characters who go about the place saying hopefully.

Neither do I wish to write about bees in general, except to say that I know they mate whilst flying, so they must be contortionists or acrobats or something, and even that depends on the drone being able to fly high enough to catch up with the queen and then he drops dead from all the exertion and the birds come and eat him up.

So there isn't much percentage in being a bee, especially if you're a worker bee, because then you don't get any fun at all, and people come and steal the honey, which is just about the same as being nationalised. So what with one thing and another you can say it's a hard life for a bee at that.

Wherefore and therefore, whilst I do not wish to write about bees as such, or bees in general, I wish to write a few words about Welsh Black bees in particular. Never mind how I first become mildly interested in the subject but, about twenty or more years ago, I am doing some research concerning the Pembrokeshire islands, and a very fine old gentleman with a great love for, and knowledge of, country matters, asks me do I ever come across anything concerning Welsh Black bees on the islands.

He has an idea that he once hears something about Welsh Black bees on Ramsey and that the last known colony of the native indigenous bees had been located on that lovely island.

I found nothing in any records and, as so often happens, was not lucky enough to ask the right questions to the right people at the right time. And those who could have told me have long since been called Home and are collecting their honey in the heather-clad hills of sunnier climes.

But, some folks reckon, Heaven won't be such a marvellous place at that if they also happen to have any Welsh Black bees there. A fearsome species, by all account. It seems there were definitely some in the Fishguard area of North Pembrokeshire over half a century ago because a chap brought his bees down with him from England, and the local bees killed the lot.

Memory plays funny tricks. I know that. And the people who do remember what happened on Ramsey have slightly differing versions. One thing I know for sure, though. The bees were put there by the late Dr. Evan Edwards, who was at that time an entomologist at the University College at Cardiff.

With the advent of war, his wife thought it would be no bad plan to keep bees to help out with the sugar ration. A friend of mine, one of her husband's colleagues, the late Dr. T. I. Davies, urged her on, and her husband also became interested.

Subsequently – and how it came about I don't know – Dr. Edwards was asked by Miss Jane Humphries, a beekeeper, of Penrhyndeudraeth, in North Wales, whether he could help to save the Welsh Back bee from extinction by taking a hive of her stock. They had been kept by her grandfather, and his grandfather before that, and way back for generations.

It seems that as a result of the ravages of the 'Isle of Wight disease' back about 1912, something like ninety percent of our own bees were wiped out and subsequently many new strains of bees were brought in from various countries. There are still, they say, a few colonies of bees to be found which carry something of the characteristics of the Welsh Black bee but, as Tom Collings, that very knowledgeable beekeeper of Ciliau Aeron says, 'How can you tell for sure? How can you prove it?'

Anyway, Dr Edwards had the rather bright idea of putting Miss Humphries' Welsh Black bees on Ramsey, and the farmer at that time, a most loveable man, the late Bertie Griffiths, was quite willing to cooperate. It would be a good place to keep the stock pure, there was plenty of heather, and it would be interesting to see whether any of them would cross to the mainland.

Round about 1948, Dr. Edwards was contemplating a future with the Ministry of Agriculture, which would have meant the NAAS. He was not too happy, however, at what was happening and took up an appointment in Ghana instead. He came back about 1962 and died the following year.

So far I have heard three versions of what happened. One is that when he came back and went to Ramsey to see about the bees, he was told that somebody had taken them away a year or two previously. He was very upset about it and never found out what became of them.

I am not much inclined to accept this version because I am assured that he never went back to Ramsey following his return from Ghana. The more likely story is that, not being any great bee-keeper, he gave it up as a bad job and destroyed the bees before he left for Ghana. Who better to remember than Dr Edwards' widow, who assured me that was so?

On the other hand, Mr. Griffiths' son Elfed, who was a boy on Ramsey at the time, assures me that the bees, considerably fewer in numbers by the end of it all, were definitely taken from the island and not destroyed there.

So what did become of the native Welsh Black bees, vicious customers that they were?

Are there any still about?

Or is it really true what it says in the Good Book that the meek shall inherit the earth?'

Western Telegraph, 8 June 1990

Perhaps it is not surprising, because there has been so much reference of late to the subject of history, that a reader has sent me a well-reasoned argument to the effect that in this computerised age of high technology there is no longer any point in young scholars having to sweat blood to learn a heap of meaningless dates. And did not the late, highly successful Henry Ford once say that History is bunk?

On the other hand I can hardly think the computer would have been developed unless there had been some knowledge of history somewhere along the line.

It started, I believe, shortly after King Harold had burned the cakes. This was several years before King Alfred shot William the Conqueror in the eye when Alfred landed at Glencoe at the time of the massacre. As dates are no longer important I can be forgiven for having forgotten this one, but I think it was round about the time of the South Sea Bubble.

King Harold's burning of the cakes, however, became a great political issue at that time because the opposition blamed it all on Benjamin Disraeli following his nationalisation of the gas industry. This was when British Gas came into being.

There was a fearful stink about it at the time when it transpired that Lloyd George, who was the leader of the Opposition, had controlling shares in the Electricity Board, and the accusation that the burning of the cakes had been caused by faulty gas burners was eventually exposed as having been the work of the dirty tricks department. This was shortly after Kim Philby had defected to Russia in an attempt to enlist the aid of Rudolph Hess but has no direct bearing on the story. It was simply that the Hanoverians thought it would be a suitable issue to introduce in an attempt to discredit the Orangemen. Grapefruit at that time had not been introduced. So, as a result of the success of the Boston Tea Party, Sir Walter Raleigh brought in several shipments of coconuts from Van Diemen's Land and this was a prelude to Edwina Currie being seconded to the Ministry of Agriculture to allay the people's serious misgivings over the outbreak of Mad Cow disease. She was not a mad cow herself. Or at least not everybody thought so. At the time she had been appointed as spokesperson for the society for the prevention of slander against Rottweillers and was the people's choice for this important new assignment with the Min. of Ag.

It was a time of great civil and religious unrest, and following the Reformation the Pope had appointed Ian Paisley, a quietly spoken Irishman, as Bishop of Durham, so Paisley immediately appointed David Jenkins as Papal nuncio. Jenkins, who was a retired sea captain, had had his (y)ear cut off by the Spaniards and this led to the Hundred Years War. At home, Jenkins used his influence to ensure that at least half the Bishops should be coloured lesbian divorcees. This was in order to maintain the political balance within the Race Relations Industry.

All this, however, is by-the-by, as we say in Pembrokeshire.

When Harold had burned the cakes Queen Boadicea gave him a right old clobbering and he went off to a cave to talk over his troubles with Robert the Bruce who had been breeding a fierce new strain of spider.

It was then that they spotted some figures and drawings which had been carved on the ceiling by Arthur Scargill when he had been organising a sit down strike of Neolithic cave-dwellers.

The only software with which they were familiar at that time was the buckskin slippers they wore in the evenings following a trying day in the hunting field. However, one evening Harold was lying in the bath looking up at the figures on the ceiling when he suddenly jumped out shouting Eureka which meant he had found it.

He had, in fact, cracked the code, as they say, and realised that these figures were details of the Poll Tax which the Vikings had introduced following the Battle of Trafalgar.

It was from these humble beginnings that technology advanced eventually to the computer as we know it today.

There is much more to it than all this, but these are the bare bones of the matter, and were it not for our knowledge of all that had happened in History previously we would still be none the wiser, and there 'tis then.

Western Telegraph, 24 July 1991

We don't seem to have heard quite so much lately about the greenhouse effect and global warning, and maybe that is not so surprising after all.

Cricket is usually reckoned to be a warm weather game, but during the first Test at Leeds there was ice on the covers. And it didn't turn out too well at Lord's either, to say nothing of the woes of the tennis enthusiasts at Wimbledon.

Down on the south coast before the floods there was a plague of octopi, if that is the plural of octopus, which normally inhabit the cold water areas. As far as I can remember the time of year was once known as Flaming June.

Somebody was telling me the other day that the scientists had measured or calculated or something, that all the ice caps had melted by goodness knows how much and the outlook for the future was rather gloomy to be sure.

Of course, it could be that this melting process has been going on even longer than that, but the scientists didn't have the equipment to measure it at the time.

None of it amounts to much, however, because the business about the greenhouse effect was a dead duck right from the start to anybody who knew anything about the facts of life. Like the slogan on the label of the bottle of gripe water for babbies with the wind. 'Granny told mother, and mother told me.'

At one time folks reckoned that splitting the atom had done it. Back in the thirties when they started firing from Manorbier at those targets being towed by aeroplanes there were some who said it had upset the weather pattern locally. That was before, on a wider scale, it was blamed onto all the supersonic aeroplanes that were breaking the sound barrier.

But the old timers knew better than to listen to such foolish talk.

Don't take my word for it. Go back to the newspapers in the latter half of the 19th century and you can read all about it for yourselves. There were letters all the time to explain the varying pattern of hot summers and drought, and perpetual rain and floods.

It was all caused by the coming of the railways. All the steam and the vibration, and all this and that and one thing and another which any fool was capable of understanding.

Now this greenhouse effect, which was caused by the environmentally unfriendly motor cars upsetting the ozone layer, seems to have levelled out and the weather is back to normal. So, what do the politicians do?

As always, they move too late and then get it all wrong anyway. They plan to plough millions and billions and trillions of pounds of other people's money into driving all the cars off the road and opening up the railways on a scale hitherto unknown to homo sapiens. Who was it said that all we ever learn from history is that we never learn from history? Or something like that.

The effects this will have on future weather patterns are almost too horrendous to contemplate. So don't let anybody say they haven't been warned. And long years ago, when I started in this columnar business, a wise old editor said never to forget that talk of the weather was always a sure winner, and there 'tis then.

Western Telegraph, 7 **August 1991**

Did you read about that 12,000-year-old carcass of a mastodon which had been dug up recently from a peat bog in Ohio, America? The mastodon, in case you didn't know, was the ancestor of the elephant.

The carcass had been so well preserved that the spear marks inflicted by primitive man were clearly visible in the area of the ribs. The conclusion of the investigating professors and what-not is that the hunters drove this poor old heffalump into the peat bog where his feet became stuck, and then he was speared to death while helpless.

So it is beginning to look as if man has always been a bit of a hunter, and there was no League Against Cruel Sports in those days to call upon the hunters to desist from such nefarious practices. And fox-hunting, as far as I know, had not been invented.

A casual passing reference such as this should ensure at least half-a-dozen letters from irate readers. It would help the Editor no end during what is known in the newspaper world as the silly season which is now approaching. [Letters should be kept as brief as possible and be written on one side of the paper only.]

Of more immediate concern, however, is the advice currently being given in case of an attack by a Rottweiler or pit bull terrier or some such.

Myself when young oft'times received the advice of what to do in the event of being bitten by a ferret. It was to insert the index finger of the free hand with some force up the rectum of the animal when it would immediately be prevailed upon to let go. That was not exactly how the advice was worded, but it is the best translation which comes to mind as being suitable for a family paper.

Fortunately, the emergency never arose when it would have been found necessary to apply this particular remedy, but it was always something of a comfort to know that it sounded like a reasonable possibility.

Howsomever, I am rather less sanguine about the same advice now being peddled on what remedial action to take in the event of being set upon by one of the unmuzzled canines reported to be roaming the land at will to the danger of one and all. The advice has been modified in this case, however, to using a walking-stick which has to be inserted up the anus of the ravening brute.

I must confess to being somewhat puzzled as to who will provide the walking-stick, and who will do the inserting, assuming that the person being savaged is in no fit state to do so. Furthermore, in an age when an old gentleman who defends himself against a young roughneck who is attacking him with a knife, can be arrested by the police and charged with assault, the Rottweiler and pit bull terrier could be on to a good thing. You can be reasonably sure that there would soon be somebody from the ranks of you-know-who to start shouting the odds to the effect that the Rottweiler or pit bull terrier had become the injured party. No doubt much would depend on the type of walking-stick used.

A banner-waving demonstration could then be organised. [Letters should be etc. etc.]

So, what with and one thing and another, I reckon we're living in funny old times at that, and there 'tis then.

Western Telegraph, 18 December 1991

With the fox-hunting season here once again we must address ourselves to the many aspects of all that is involved.

It is not easy to suggest an answer acceptable to everybody, but I believe I can go some way towards it.

It is well-known that once upon a time dogs are very wild creatures to be sure. Then man decided to domesticate them and train them for hunting and retrieving, and digging into the bowels of the earth with their busy little forepaws, or carrying casks of brandy and pulling small milk carts and one thing and another.

Now as time goes by it becomes evident that when these dogs are not out hunting or retrieving or digging holes or carrying casks of brandy or pulling milk carts, they do nothing with more enthusiasm than fouling the pavements.

In fact this has now become a great concern for one and all and mind you don't step in it. And if the dogs are not doing it on the pavements, they are doing it on the beaches and, if you don't step in it either you or the children could be unlucky enough to roll in it.

COLLARS

According to many characters who go round with their placards hollering stinking fish and all this and that, foxes are very noble, loving, gentle and harmless creatures to be sure, and in fact, if the truth could be told, are very nearly man's best friend.

The answer is therefore obvious. We must go back to the beginning and start to domesticate the foxes. Mark you, it might well take a little time, but the result could be so spectacular that it could be worth the effort.

Eventually the foxes will have collars and leads so that their loving owners can walk them along the pavements, the collars being fitted with little bells to warn the dogs that the foxes are coming and, as the foxes are now man's best friend, the dogs will know to depart in haste and the pavements and beaches will be kept clean.

Having learned from the mistakes of his ancestors, man will have trained the sweet-smelling foxes not to do their little tootsies-woopsies on the pavements, and it will be very pleasant for one and all.

There is only one small snag to all this which will have been recognised by the more intelligent reader, and that is that all the dogs will have to hide somewhere out of the way of the foxes.

So the foxes will then have to be trained to become very fearsome and go out in search of the dogs which by this time will have reverted to type and become wilder than somewhat, and the erstwhile Master of Fox Hounds will then become Master of Hound Foxes.

MOGGIES

The descendants of them what used to holler stinking fish can then get out their ancestors' scarves and duffel coats and placards and demonstrate as in days of yore.

The foxes will also go in pursuit of all the moggies in sight and these creatures will be eliminated from the face of the earth. The RSPB will no doubt be pleased to give a donation in support of this work so that all the merry song birds will be able to sing tweet-tweet and make as much mess on your window sills as the dogs used to make on the pavements.

There could be a superabundance of rats and mice once we have lost our lovely pussycats, so we shall either have to bring back the terriers or train the intelligent foxes to go out and catch these vermin so that they can be put in cages and sold as pets.

I am not sure how this will relate to the greenhouse effect in a National Park, but it's worth a thought, and there 'tis then.

Western Telegraph, 1 April 1992

Ever been to a wedding? You don't go to many these days, what with all the talk of live-in partners and shacking up and one thing and another. There don't seem to be all that many weddings about.

So maybe that accounts for it. The photographers I mean. They have to try to make a bit of hay while the sun is shining. Or, to put it another way, the time to kill the fly is when he's in the sugar basin.

How did they manage in days of yore? Gramfer and Granny had some tidy pictures, standing there alongside the aspidistra, with one of them in the high-backed chair, without all the current nonsense.

In the old days the wedding day was the big day for the bride. But not any more. That idea is very old hat. The wedding day now is strictly for the photographer. Amazing, is it not, that with all the modern technology the job seems to take longer and longer? And sometimes in fact even longer than that.

Like one day last summer. A nice wedding it was, too. At 11.30 a.m. Nice vicar. All very reverent and dignified and prayerful and everything as it should be. And no pictures in the church please, and there will be time for all the pictures you care to take outside afterwards.

So we left them to it and set off for the wedding reception with time to spare, and called in at the hospital in passing to see a lonely poor old soul who was on his own, and we reckoned to give him fifteen or twenty minutes.

Well, you know, and I should have known, that things do not always work out like that, and we finished up by staying for much more than half-an-hour. And by that time, of course, we were late for the wedding reception, weren't we?

So I put my foot down, as the saying is, and didn't make many friends on the way as far as I know, and reached the appointed venue, only to find that we'd turned up at the wrong place because there was nobody there. But the head boss man of the outfit said not to worry as that was the right place, but the meal had been booked for 4.00 p.m. because the young lady photographer had taken the wedding party off to some sequestered glade for some more pictures to be taken. And I said he had to be joking, and he said he'd never been more serious in all his so-and-so life, and what did I know about that.

Mark you, we were luckier than the rest of them because we had cousins staying at the joint and they had a room with all this and that en-suite, and a contraption to make a cup of coffee. Eventually the young couple and their entourage arrived, but this was by no means the end of the suffering, because one and all then had to turn out in twenty-seven different positions and poses before the hunger could be assuaged. It is, so the connoisseurs tell me, known as the danger hour, because this is when the young bloods have too much to drink on empty stomachs and then proceed to make fools of themselves and spoil the day for everybody else. This did not happen on this occasion because they were not that type. They just sank deeper and deeper into their misery.

It turned out afterwards that in the fullness of time the young couple were offered one hundred and goodness-knows how many pictures out of which they could select twenty, as far as I could gather, for whatever the price was that the young lady quoted.

Now that the fox-hunting and shooting seasons are over, I should be more than happy to second the motion if some fellow sufferer would care to propose open season on the most unfeeling of wedding photographers. I reckon the guests are entitled to some small consideration, too. And whilst it is very nice to have a reminder of a precious occasion, there is, as the old timers used to say, a difference between scratching your backside and tearing the skin off, except that they didn't say backside, and there 'tis then.

---

2 August 1956

The whole story

A farmer was digging a hole in a field. He'd just finished when his neighbour came along and said he'd like to have it, so he sold it to him. So then he started digging another and his other neighbour came along and the same thing happened again. Well, in the end all his neighbours had bought holes off him, and this farmer thought he was on to a good thing. So he thought he'd really cash in on it. After all was said and done, times were bad, government no good, potatoes still in the ground, cows going dry, hens stopped laying, corn battered down in the storm, and a heap more besides. So he dug a lot of holes all over the place, loaded them up on the tractor and trailer and drove them down to the mart. When he reached the mart-ground there was a bloke there from the Min. of Ag. and Fish (and Food) who was writing out permits for different things. So he stops this farmer and he says: "What you got there?" and the farmer says, "A load of holes." And this bloke says, "What you going to do with 'em?" "I'm going to sell 'em," says the farmer. "Anything wrong with that?" "Yes," says the bloke from the Ministry. "Plenty. You'd be a wholesaler without a licence."

Western Telegraph, 22 July 1992

Interesting it is indeed to read of the recent recommendations of that ridiculous quango known as the Countryside Commission in their objective to turn the country into one big rural museum where the denizens of the towns and cities may roam at will.

It is known as Countryside Stewardship and must be a delight to the politicians.

One idea is to restore and conserve the old strip farm systems. Splendid idea, but we must hope that it will not stop at that.

Some years ago, when the emphasis was all on efficiency and increased production from the land, I remember that eminent agriculturalist, the late Rex Paterson, telling me a story of how he had bought a farm from an old chap who had been born on the farm, as had his father before him.

Within a matter of a couple of months Rex found it necessary to widen the gateway into one particular field, so the old stone gatepost was yanked out and a very workmanlike job was made of widening the gateway.

And, just as the improvement was being completed, the old chap who had retired to live in a house nearby, came along and, in great admiration, said what a splendid job it was, and added for good measure: 'We always got stuck in that old gateway with the gambo at haymaking as far back as I can remember, even in Gramfer's time.'

NOSTALGIC

So I hope that replacing the old stone gateposts and narrowing the gateways will be high on the list of priorities.

I wouldn't suggest that farmers revert to milking by hand, but they should certainly get rid of the bulk milk tankers and go back to the ten gallon churns which now seem to be used only outside Ye Olde Cottage as flower pots, evocative of days of yore. Most nostalgic they are.

While we are at it we should also demolish all the modern milking parlours and return to using the old-fashioned cowsheds, and this would soon eliminate the need for milk quotas.

Such ploughing as is done at all should be done by horses drawing a single furrow plough, unless the farmer should prove to be really enthusiastic and opt to push the old-fashioned breast plough himself.

Corn, where any is grown, should be sown by hand, as in Biblical days when the sower went forth sowing. Likewise harvesting should be by sickle, and fertiliser, if used at all, should be spread by hand from the old seed-lip.

It would be a sure way of putting an end to allegations of pollution of the rivers from excessive use of fertilisers! Most certainly corn drills and seed drills would be de trop as the French say, and we might as well say it now that we are in Europe, whatever that is supposed to mean.

SLOGANS

The fact that all this would have a disastrous knock-on effect and put thousands and thousands of town and city dwellers out of work is neither here nor there.

What is more, it should not be too long before the indigenous trees would be growing all over the place every which way once more and obviating the need for such slogans as 'Save A Tree.'

Interpretive literature will be necessary, and I am more than willing to help with that. We must also have such notices as Ye Crowe Nests Here by ye olde oak tree, and Here Be Hartebeests in the occasional field just to fool the townies into thinking that they are not looking at any ordinary old cow.

The permutations and possibilities are endless, but one thing is for sure. There will be no more nonsense talk about set-aside and all the rest of it, and we shall be producing precious little food.

What sense this makes in a world where more than half the people are starving is more than I can tell you, but I suppose that is a subject to be left to other quangos and politicians, and there 'tis then.

Western Telegraph, 23 December 1992

It was just a routine visit to the doctor's surgery for a flu jab, as I believe it is commonly known.

Well, you don't expect to be able to go in straightaway because there are other characters who also have to sit there waiting their turn, and what is more natural than to start chatting about this and that and one thing and another and where do you come from?

There is a young gentleman sitting next to me who is also waiting for a flu jab, and on top of that he does not look any too full of the joys of spring and this is not surprising because it turns out that he has kidney trouble and is on one of these machines.

He is ahead of me in the queue, but before his turn comes we are joined by a very sprightly lady who does not look as if she is in any need of a doctor whatsoever. And it turns out that she has been waiting for a long time in the wrong place and now will have to start waiting all over again, and furthermore she is ninety two years of age.

So, like I said, there is now some more chat and she explains that, although she lives much of her life in England, she is Welsh by birth. Her late husband had been a miner and during the General Strike in 1926 she lives in Aberdare and is six months without money.

It is reasonable to ask in the face of such statements how do you survive, and she says well everybody in the street sets off to the north to go begging and then they come back and share out everything between the rest of them.

Now this strikes me as being very great hardship indeed, but the lady smiles and says oh, no, those times were much better because people were not for ever demanding more of this and more of that, and forever having to have something new, and it simply doesn't matter. No indeed, she says again, it doesn't matter.

They had time to count their many blessings, and then I remember there is a very fine old Sankey hymn on this subject.

At this stage somebody says next please, and the young gentleman who has the kidney trouble and is anxious to get home insists that the old lady must go in ahead of him, which is a reassuring gesture indeed in an age when chivalry is reckoned to be dead and when every day we come across much evidence of great selfishness in many places.

When she departs the young gentleman says that he knows he cannot expect to live to such a great age, and then we are joined by a young couple, married nice and tidy, which is also refreshing in the times in which we live, and they have a lovely little baby girl of a year old.

The old lady then comes back and her face lights up when she sees the little baby, because she says she has some great–grandchildren, and how old is this little baby, and good gracious there is ninety-one years between us.

So then she pulls out her purse and says she must put something in the little baby's hand, and although the young parents protest, the little old lady who has known much of deprivation in her time insists and puts a pound coin into the little baby's hand and says to her that she hopes she will never want.

Now maybe I am a bit old-fashioned, but it says in the Good Book that a little child shall lead them, and it is a time of year when we celebrate once again the birth of a very special Child with the promise of redemption for mankind.

What is more it encourages me to think that there are still characters to be found who will see beyond the tinsel and the turkey and the commercialism, and that it will really mean something special when such characters wish you a Merry Christmas, and there 'tis then.

Western Telegraph, 3 February 1992

It is a fact of life, which may or may not be known to some of you, that in my time I write many articles and even the odd book or two about the islands of Pembrokeshire. Well, now I wish to write for you about the Islets of Langerhans, but I wish to state that I do not know anything about these Islets whatsoever. Not that this matters, because many characters write on subjects of which they know nothing at all.

Now this comes about because in my old age I decide to write a novel which will make some reference to the tanning industry. But I am now so old, and it is a subject which will involve so much research, that I may not live long enough to write such a book, which is why I wish to tell you whilst I still have the chance about these Islets of Langerhans.

First of all I make some enquiries about fellmongers and tanneries and I find to my great surprise that there are now no longer any such activities in this country, and that all the skins are now sent to the Continent for curing and what do you know about that.

So I go to the library and I find a book on the subject of tanning and it is a most interesting and revealing book to be sure. It seems that in olden days it is customary for the characters who are doing the tanning to have to use what is referred to in the book as dog dung.

Now this reminds me of the lady who complains to her neighbour that her husband is always on about manure for the garden, which causes her great embarrassment, so her neighbour says to get him to call it fertiliser, and the lady says it has taken her twenty-five years to get him to say manure. It also says in this book that, if they do not fancy using dog dung, then they may wish to use pigeon dung, so maybe it is not surprising that there are no longer any tanneries to be found.

Even so, as I explain for you in this column recently, there is now a great call for diversification, and there is no shortage of the old raw material, by whatever name you wish to call it, and if you will care to take a stroll along the seafront at Amroth you will see exactly what I mean because the raw material is there in abundance, and in all different colours according to whatever is the latest pet food on which the creators, or depositors as you might say, have been fed, and mind you don't step in it.

This comes about because many subjects bring their dogs to Amroth in large numbers to bark upon the beach to the annoyance of the native population, or to do their tootsy-woopsies on the pavement, but the locals do not by any manner or means refer to it as tootsy-woopsies.

Personally speaking, I cannot see ADAS recommending grants for using this as a raw material, but it is possible that this SPARC* outfit, who take great delight in handing out our money, may wish to give grants for characters to set up some tanneries here and there, and this brings me back to the book which I find in the library. And it says in this book that where characters are a bit queasy in the old stomach, and do not like the idea of coming to Amroth to scrape up the raw material off the pavement, but still wish to set up in the tannery business, they may decide to use pancreatic juice or minced pancreas.

Now it seems that the pancreas, which the butchers call 'sweetbreads', is a gland situated near the liver and the duodenum, and if you will look in a good medical book you will find that this is where these Islets of Langerhans are situated.

So there you are, and here I am, and even if I do not live long enough to find out all there is to know about tanneries and their requirements by way of raw materials in order to write my best-selling novel, at least I have been able to explain to you about the Islets of Langerhans, and there 'tis then.

---

* SPARC: South Pembrokeshire Partnership for Action with Rural Communities. A mercifully short-lived organisation, which became a joke in Pembrokeshire, backed by public money, much of which was wasted on ridiculous schemes, mostly of no benefit to anybody.

Western Telegraph, 16 June 1993

Maybe you will recall that some time ago I mention the fact that I am thinking in terms of writing a best-selling novel, which will make some reference in passing to the tanning industry, and how characters in days of old are in the habit of using dog dung in conjunction with same.

Now, of course, anybody who knows anything about such matters will understand that this will be only a small part of the story, and there are many other interesting matters which happen at the time when the story will take place.

So I decide to go to The Welsh Folk Museum at St Fagans, which is a most interesting place to be sure, to fill in on a bit of the old background which will be helpful in the preparation of this great work, and this is known in the trade as research.

And as I already make this discovery about dogs and the old whatnot in conjunction with the tanning industry, I decide to take a little look at the dogs working on the treadmills, one on the butter churn, and one turning the roast beef on the spit in the kitchen. In fact, I remember seeing these exhibits many years ago and they are very interesting to be sure.

STUFFED

I hope and trust, however, that you will realise that these dogs are nothing but stuffed dogs, and only poor old mongrels at that. But I do not expect that the fact that they are poor old mongrels will affect the quality of the butter or the roast beef, or not that much anyway.

Now I know that these stuffed dogs are there for many years, but although I am prepared to find that maybe they have become a little moth-eaten since I last see them, I am more surprised than somewhat to discover that they are no longer there at all. So I ask some questions and eventually it transpires that they are removed because they offend the sensitivities of them that do not like the idea of dogs ever having been used for such purposes, so maybe these sensitive souls are like Mr Stalin and such characters who think they can re-write history. But I do not discover to which branch of the Animal Rights outfit they belong.

I hope and trust, however, that they do not hear the broadcast on the wireless on April 1st when a character from the north of Pembrokeshire explains how he has started milking some seals, and what a profitable business he is making of it.

What does not come out on this broadcast, however, is that this character is slaughtering the surplus seals and skinning them and selling the skins for the making of leather harnesses.

MARKET

Furthermore it seems that he also has a ready market lined up for the seal meat, which at the moment is going into the deep-freeze. Apparently, with the closing down of Brawdy, the place will now be used as a resettlement area for Hong Kong Chinese, and it is a fact which is well known to one and all that the Chinese are decidedly partial to a mouthful or two of the old frozen seal meat, and all manner of other such tasty morsels besides.

Come to think of it, I hear tell when I am young that the Chinese are not averse to a spot of the old dog meat either. And whilst I am also told of many characters who are known to partake of a slice of dog meat in times of old when the economy is much worse than it is now, even though they do not live as far away from here as the Chinese, I do not do any research on the subject, and I wish to state that I do not intend to make any reference to such in my best-selling novel.

The only thing which is troubling me is the thought that, with all this talk of the Chinese and their culinary tastes, it would be a sin and a shame, to say nothing of a mean and dirty trick at that, if indeed some nefarious character had nicked the poor old stuffed mongrels and flogged them to some unsuspecting Chinaman, and there 'tis then.

---

9 February 1956

Tea Total

The story goes that when all the farmers were in London a week or two ago for the annual meeting of the National Farmers' Union one of the company stayed at an hotel that prided itself on the excellence of its service.

First morning at breakfast the waiter asked whether he would like tea or coffee. This is nothing like the story where the waiter asked if he'd like a serviette and the farmer said: "No thanks, I never did care much for the old things." So the farmer said he'd have tea.

"China, Indian or Ceylon ?" asked the waiter.

"China."

"Black, green or mixed?"

"Black."

"Pekoe, Souchong or Foochow?" came back the waiter.

"Pekoe."

"Orange, Broken Orange or Flowering Orange?"

"Orange Pekoe," said the farmer, and thought he'd won.

The waiter smiled and asked, "Milk, cream or lemon?"

"Milk," said the farmer.

"Jersey, Guernsey or Shorthorn?"

But the farmer kept Friesians, so he changed his mind quick and said: "I'll have coffee and I'll have it whichever way you make it."

Of course, the story mightn't be true.

Western Telegraph, 9 **March 1994**

Now that the back to basics* joke has reached its sell-by date, there can hardly be much mileage in it for those who seek to contribute to a column such as this. But hopefully I can be said to have a safe pair of hands, and I think I may say I can field any questions which may come my way on the subject. Nor would I seek to stone-wall them. Hopefully.

Hopefully there must be somebody out there who will wish to monitor this quantum leap. This is not an expression which has anything to do with a politician jumping into bed. It is merely another way of saying that you are getting your act together and want people to think that you know what you are talking about when it comes to the bottom line.

I hear what you say because you must remember I have been into this columnar business a long time, and I know how to test the temperature of the water. I would not seek to set myself up as a role model, but I am usually conscious of any sea change and quick to detect if there is a ground-swell of opinion. What is more, I have a pretty fair track record, right across the spectrum, particularly in an environmental context.

This is not quite the same as saying that I wish to draw a line under it, but hopefully we are singing from the same hymn sheet in a very real sense. Hopefully.

It is, I believe, received opinion that in this columnar business there has to be a degree of forward planning, and it needs to be a whole new ball game on a level playing field, otherwise the Editor will show the contributor the red card. That is when he has to bite the bullet. (The contributor, not the Editor.) Then hopefully the ball is in somebody else's court. Hopefully. Period. End of story.

These are some of the reasons why I feel that it is down to me to up-date you in a meaningful way on an escalating situation which needs to be beefed up. Indeed, if I may say so, it is a key factor in establishing the pecking order. At the end of the day, anyone who is in the business of looking for a knee-jerk reaction has to have a cutting edge. Without it, he would have no clout whatsoever. Not even nice Mr Major.

These indeed are the nuts and bolts which have to be taken on board, totally, and the icon of a quantum leap. A columnist has it all to do in an ongoing situation and has to go right up to the wire. Anything else is a dead duck, and you can quote me on that as well. Hopefully.

In a word, therefore, what we should be saying is that, whilst we have to stand up to be counted, it is the ultimate obscenity at grassroots level in a caring society if the lads are not allowed to play it by ear when they take the litmus test, especially when they have it all to do. That is a proven syndrome.

In targeting this issue, eyeball-to-eyeball, which many sound judges regard as a different animal, synchronised transitional flexibility can never be a satisfactory alternative to replace the proven qualities of any functional intermental concept until we can get it up and running. And, basics or not, at the end of the day, that's the name of the game. If not, I think we should be told, and there 'tis then.

---

* 'Back to Basics' was an ill-fated attempt in 1993 to restore some credibility to the John Major government in such matters as law and order, education, and public probity, following so many revelations of extra-marital affairs and financial chicanery involving politicians. It was also during the premiership of John Major that, in 1997, the Milk Marketing Board, which had been the salvation of farming in the 1930s, was abolished.

Western Telegraph, 30 March 1994

There has been much talk in political circles lately on the subject of question and answer, and when is a truth a half-truth, and when is it nothing like the truth, and which half of the answer are you supposed to believe, if any of it, and so on and so forth, and who is expected to know the difference? And who would take the word of a politician anyway?

Since as far back as I can remember I have never had any time for politicians, of any party whatsoever, in any manner shape or form and, if you think that sounds like a harsh judgement, let me quote for you what the Patron Saint of writers had to say on the subject.

The Patron Saint of writers, in case you didn't happen to know, was St. Francis De Sales, who was born in Savoy more than four hundred years ago. Eventually he became Bishop of Geneva, where these days politicians tend to hold the occasional conference in order to draw their travelling expenses, like County Councillors and all the countless millions and trillions of bureaucrats and other such characters, so maybe St. Francis was a man before his time at that.

St. Francis' great companion was Jean Pierre Camus, Bishop of Belley, and it is to him we are indebted for having recorded so much of the Saint's thinking.

On one occasion Camus expressed his surprise to St. Francis that the Duke of Savoy, who was one of the most excellent princes and foremost statesmen of his time, should never have employed St. Francis in his affairs, especially in those which concerned France, as they were not very prosperous. And Camus gave as his reasons for expressing this surprise the fact that he considered St. Francis De Sales to be a man of such gentleness, patience and skill, which were always certain to bring about the desired result.

St. Francis heard his friend out patiently, then replied, 'You exaggerate and say too much. You imagine that others esteem me as you do – you who are always looking at me through a magnifying glass. Nevertheless, as far as our Prince is concerned, my feeling is quite different from yours. For I believe that he shows very good judgement in this matter.

Why do I think this? Well, in the first place, I certainly do not have that skill in the directing of political affairs which you think I have. Is it at all likely that I should? In fact, the very words *business, human prudence, politics,* and the like, terrify me. And this is not all. Frankly, I know nothing of the art of lying or pretence, which are the chief instruments of political diplomacy. Not for the province of Savoy, nor even of the entire empire, would I be able to take part in deceit.

My dealings with people are always honest, simple and in good faith. My words are the outcome of the thoughts of my heart. I cannot put on a double face, and I hate duplicity with a mortal hatred, knowing that God holds the deceitful man in abomination. Not many who know me fail to discover at least this much of my character. Hence, they judge wisely when they say that I am not suited for a business in which one must speak peace to one's neighbour while at the same time plot against him. Furthermore, I have always followed that heavenly maxim of the Apostle 'No man being a soldier to God entangleth himself with secular business that he may please Him to Whom he hath engaged himself.'

It is a well-known fact that I am never likely to become a Saint, even with a very small 's'. So you do not have to take my word for it about politicians, but I thought you might be interested in what the head boss of our lot had to say about them over four hundred years ago, and if it was good enough for him to think it, then it's good enough for me, and there 'tis then.

Western Telegraph, 8 June 1994

Maybe you read recently that the RSPB now has a plan which will create 65 jobs in the Land of Our Fathers. They will do this, apparently, by employing people to go round with maps and interpretive literature, and all this and that saying ye olde kite nesteth here and please to come and learn all about it.

It is now generally accepted that it is a noble ideal to make work for people, and if you happen to think that, then I suggest you come in with your muddy boots and walk all over the kitchen floor just after the good lady of the house has washed it, and then ask her opinion on the subject unless, as is more than likely, she gives you her opinion without your having to wait for it.

As I have previously opined in this column, the RSPB is now just about on a par, in the minds of those who know how many beans make five, with that other self-perpetuating bureaucracy, the RSPCA.

You do not need to be told that, by this reference to the red kite, the scene of the action will be in the upper reaches of the Towy Valley. Until now, the idea has always been that everything must be very hush-hush, and do not thou by any means seek to wander wither these characters wouldst thou should not. So what is going to happen now with the disturbance to all the other little dicky birds that go tweet-tweet with their merry song in springtime?

HAVOC

The trouble is with these characters who have this interest in nature and so-called conservation, they seem to think that the whole of nature is their own private and special domain as if by divine right.

And if you missed the bit about employing 65 people in the land of the red kite, then maybe you have read the more often publicised stories of the havoc being wrought by the cormorants which have now moved to inland waters and are playing merry what's-it all round amongst the trout ponds and rivers.

Many of you, I suspect, will be old enough to remember that not so long ago the Ministry of Agriculture, Fisheries of Food used to pay a bounty of a shilling a beak, I think it was, to shoot these piscatorial predators.

And do you know what happens now? Before fishermen can shoot them, they have to have a licence, and all because of the nonsense being promulgated by the RSPB.

EUPHORIC

I believe I have quoted for you before now the wisdom of the little cloth-capped Welshman, who joined the train at Cardiff on an occasion when I was homeward bound from London, and between there and Port Talbot expounded on the follies of mankind (it was before the age of political correctness). And his parting shot was, 'We must be God's chosen people, boyo, because nobody else could be so bloody stupid and get away with it.'

All is not lost, however, and I am not without hope, because I see that a Mr Ian Bell has now moved from being cautiously euphoric to saying that we must stand up and shout in order to attract the tourists. It is not enough apparently to print another couple of hundred thousand guides and give them away even though nobody is ever likely to read them. What we have to do is stand up and shout.

I do not know how this advice will go down with the 65 characters who are explaining about the red kite, but maybe it will be considered a good idea if it is done every time you see a cormorant.

Chairman Mao, I believe, when he wanted to rid China of small birds, ordered everybody to stand outside and clap their hands in the belief that the birds would keep on flying round and about and every which way until they all dropped dead from exhaustion.

I do not know whether you ever try clapping your hands or shouting at a cormorant, but personally I think it will be much more effective to let him have both barrels, and preferably loaded with heavy duck shot at that, and there 'tis then.

Western Telegraph, 20 July 1994

No sooner have the dire warnings about the greenhouse effect and global warming been exposed as being strictly the old phonus bolonus, than that useless quango known as the Countryside Commission wheels out a professor to predict doom and devastation by the year 2050, so maybe I should be grateful that I shall not be here to have to write about it.

More pests will be migrating to the countryside, this professor says, just as if we do not have enough two-legged pests about already.

Meanwhile, the Council for the Protection of Rural England, the rich man's equivalent of the Council for the Protection of Rural Wales, deplores the fact that all and sundry are being encouraged to descend on the rural areas in great numbers to create leisure centres and theme parks and such.

The people who encourage all this, they say, are the English Tourist Board, who will be the rich man's equivalent of the Welsh Tourist Board. It is well-known that these are noble-minded characters who are by no means in it for what they can get out of it, and are most wise and diligent at all times. In fact, I am told the other day that they are so wise and diligent that a statistician has calculated that, for every thousand pounds they spend on publicity, one thousand fewer people come to Wales. So maybe some people will be pleased about the result of their efforts at that.

Those of you who are young enough to be worried by all this drivel about global warming and rising water levels may take comfort from the fact that another professor points out that, if you take so much ice and put it in a bucket and melt it, you will find that the water level does not alter. Howsomever, amidst all the plethora of advice and opinions emanating from experts various, one little ray of light has reached the dark places of my mind.

It happens a while ago when I am coming back from the island of Caldey, and on the boat there is a character with whom I have a little chat about one thing and another in a manner which is reckoned to be civil and polite, as is the custom on such occasions. This character is maybe a bit special because he tells me that he is an authority on birds, and this is very interesting because I am always anxious and willing to learn from characters who know more than I do on any subject whatsoever.

Now this character is not only an expert on birds, but he has his binoculars and camera, and woollen stockings and heavy lace-up boots, and a couple of bird books to prove it, to say nothing of the fact that he has a very smart badge to certify that he is a fully paid-up member of the RSPB, and this impresses me above a bit.

Well, he can see that I am greatly interested in all he has to tell me, so then he waxes enthusiastic and explains that his day has been very rewarding because he sees a pair of black swans. Now I have been sculling around these parts for a long time, but I never see or hear tell of any black swans about the place. I hear many of the stories about the black monk on Caldey, but I know they are strictly the old phonus bolonus, just like the stories of the global warming, so I ask this character where exactly on Caldey does he see these black swans, and he says he does not see them on Caldey, but flying across towards that island over there. And you know, and I know, that the island over there is St Margaret's Island where there are cormorants in great numbers.

So maybe if this character is in good standing with the RSPB it explains why they are so anxious to protect the cormorants if they think they are black swans.

So now we know, and don't forget that this is where you read it first, and there 'tis then.

Western Telegraph, 12 October 1994

If you are an avid reader of this publication you will no doubt have read on the Letters Page a little while ago a cry from the heart of some well-meaning character who wishes everybody to become vegetarians.

If you tend to be more selective, then maybe you missed it, and you can take my word for it that you didn't miss much.

The idea seems to be that, if everybody answers the call, we shall all live longer and there will be no need to slaughter all the beautiful animals which God put there in the first place for the purpose, because He had not read any letters in this paper saying how wicked it all is and also how unhealthy. This is known, apparently, as Animal Aid.

I don't know how you think, but when I look round and see all the mayhem and skulduggery which is going on all over the place generally, I tend to go along with those who say they are very glad they lived when they did, and they do not see any great percentage in living all that much longer anyway.

Furthermore, the general idea seems to be that people are already living longer, and there are far too many old people about, without adding further to the troubles of the younger generation in having to support them, especially with the economy in the state it is, and with millions and trillions of bureaucrats to be kept in the manner to which they have become accustomed. And we have to die from something sometime anyway, and so what?

I already live to a great age, and I eat my way through my share of all sorts of meat in my time, and also many other things which are supposed to be bad for the constitution, as well as washing it all down with the odd bottle, and on the rare occasions when I have to see the doctor, if I happen to sneeze or something really frightening and serious like that, he puts that thing round my arm and pumps it up and says good gracious your blood pressure is most satisfactory, and what is the reason? So then I have to tell him that I use hardly any salt, and that I have a very placid temperament to be sure.

As far as the animals are concerned, I remember a joke on the back of a matchbox many years ago, and maybe even longer than that. And the joke is about one old drunk talking to another old drunk, and he says that every year a female crocodile lays ten thousand eggs, and the second old drunk says 'Ish that sho?' And then the first old drunk goes on to say that every year the male crocodile comes along and eats up nine thousand nine hundred and ninety nine of the eggs. And the second old drunk says, 'Who caresh?' And the first old drunk says, 'I do. Otherwishe we'd be hip-deep in crocodilesh'.

Well, as you can guess, the character who is writing about saving all the animals from slaughter does not say what we will have to do with them after we save them, and who is going to look after them and feed them, unless we appoint some more bureaucrats, because it stands to reason we cannot expect all the wicked and cruel farmers to look after them if the wicked and cruel farmers cannot hope to make something out of it.

Apart from the fact that the figures quoted about the so-called bad eating habits and the death rate, and all the rest of it, have long since been exposed as a heap of nonsense, I would only seek to mention in passing that at one time I am friendly with a character who makes a very good living running a health food shop which supplies all the right things to the dedicated and earnest types who go in for this sort of thing in a big way, and it is interesting indeed to study them and the clothes they wear and the way they dress, and so on and so forth. They are all devoted and committed vegetarians.

Then, one day, I happen to mention to this friend of mine the question of staff, and he smiles and says he does not have any trouble at all. Then he smiles some more and says that at one time he tries employing some of these vegetarians, but he does not employ any of them these days, and I ask him why is this and he says, 'Good God, man, the buggers were nearly falling asleep behind the counter half the time.'

And whilst I am not saying that I approve of such language, it is only right and proper that I should tell it to you just as the man told it to me, and there 'tis then.